Waterways

By Steam Launch through Ireland

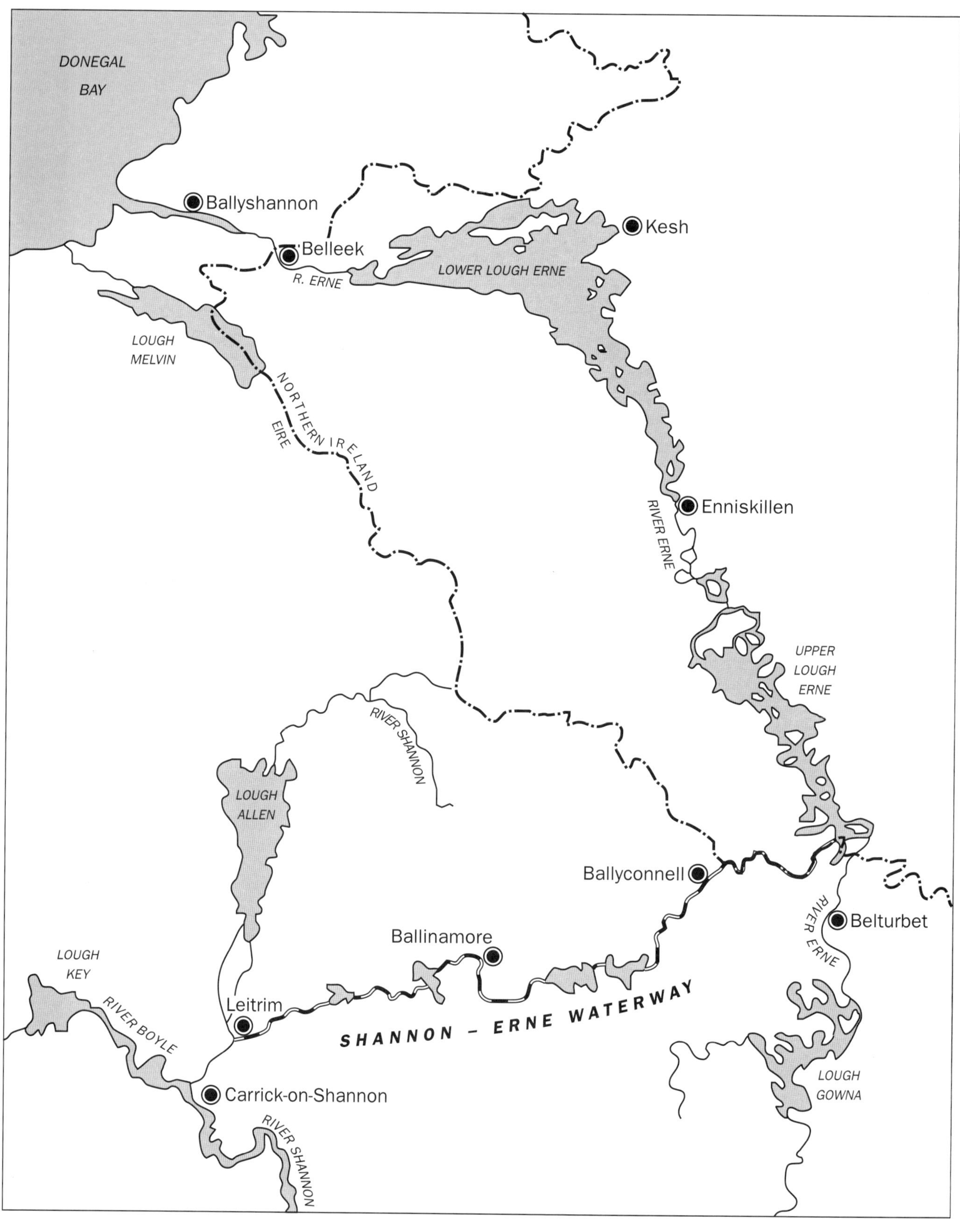

DONEGAL BAY
Ballyshannon
Belleek
R. ERNE
Kesh
LOWER LOUGH ERNE
LOUGH MELVIN
NORTHERN IRELAND
EIRE
RIVER ERNE
Enniskillen
UPPER LOUGH ERNE
RIVER SHANNON
LOUGH ALLEN
Ballyconnell
RIVER ERNE
Belturbet
LOUGH KEY
Ballinamore
RIVER BOYLE
Leitrim
SHANNON – ERNE WATERWAY
LOUGH GOWNA
Carrick-on-Shannon
RIVER SHANNON

Waterways

By Steam Launch through Ireland

Dick Warner

with Niall Fallon

BOXTREE

First published in Great Britain in 1995
by Boxtree Limited

Other photographs kindly supplied by: Belleek
China, p.143; Brendan Campbell, pp.67, 101, 117;
ESB International, p.22; Gaelic Athletic Association,
p.29; Hare Krishnas, p.80; Northern Ireland Tourist
Board, pp. 55, 66, 79, 86, 91, 126, 127, 129, 131;
Riversdale House, p.39; Rogan's of Ballyshannon,
pp.132, 133, 137; Vanity Fair (1880), p.97

1 2 3 4 5 6 7 8 9 10

Designed by Geoff Hayes
Printed and bound in the UK by Bath Press
Colourbooks for

Boxtree Limited
Broadwall House
21 Broadwall
London   SE1 9PL

ISBN 1 85283 934 1

A CIP catalogue entry for this book is available from
the British Library

Acknowledgements
Many thanks to David Laing, Declan Kearney, Anne
Marie Fitzpatrick, Maria Anderton, all at Emdee
Productions, Ruth Heard, OPW, ESB, Lowe Alpine,
Fermanagh District Council, Western Marine,
BallyKeeran Cruisers, Bord na Mona and Northern
Ireland Tourist Board

Contents

I have travelled to an extent which some people might envy. I have explored the yellow deserts of Botswana and the white deserts of Greenland; wheezed, with smoker's lungs, up mountains from the Rockies to the Himalayas and canoed in County Cavan.

I have also often wondered why I do it. Some of it has been for business, some for recreation, but most of it has been uncomfortable and even occasionally dangerous. If I turn to cliché for an answer to the question I find that travel 'broadens the mind', is 'a drug' and is 'the best education in the world'. None of this is really satisfactory. And I find, as I get older, that my travel appetites are changing. The exotic is losing its appeal. The nomad itch is still there but I'm able to scratch it nearer home.

In 1991 I made one of the most profoundly important journeys of my life – from Dublin to Limerick. It took ten years of planning. The background to it was that in the 1960s, while I was at school, they dismantled the inland waterways freight network in Ireland. It couldn't cope with competition from road and rail. In the 1970s I decided to settle down for a while and bought a boat, which I moored on the Grand Canal about 20 miles (32km) from Dublin and lived on. I developed an interest in the inland waterways which rapidly developed into a full-blown love affair. And an ambitious worm burrowed into my imagination and whispered to me that one last cargo should be carried by barge over the full route – from Dublin to Limerick. I should be at the helm and I should use the contacts I had in the media to finance it by filming a television documentary of the journey.

It took longer than I thought it would. I met a man called David Coote who had the barge. At the time it was the only barge in Ireland which could still motor and which had a hold which could take a cargo – all the others had been converted into houseboats and cruisers. He liked the idea. I had a friend called Tim Palmer who was a talented writer of films and another friend called Larry Masterson who was a successful independent television producer. Good ideas have to mature like good booze, and pick the right time to be consumed.

It all came together in a television documentary series called '*Waterways*'. Suddenly the promises I had made to all kinds of hard-headed people were being called in. I had to produce the goods and I realised that I wasn't sure if I could take a 50-ton boat with a primitive 1920s Bollinder semi-diesel engine and no reverse gear along 120 miles (192km) of partly disused waterway. A man called Dick Kearney and his son Declan came to my rescue. Dick is now dead and I owe him an enormous debt.

Dick Kearney had worked on the commercial boats on the inland waterways before 1960. He was a treasure-chest of knowledge, skill, patience and good humour. He took my dream on board and made it happen.

That first journey was recorded in six half-hours of television and broadcast to Ireland and nearly every country in the world. The result was astonishing. The symbolic strength, the metaphor, of a journey made with love from one mundane place to another seemed to strike a chord which resonated across cultures. It had a lot to do with the professional skills of the team who made the programmes. It had even more to do with the metaphor.

When the hard-nose of the media blunders into success it has one Pavlovian response … the sequel. *Waterways 2* was a journey along the Shannon – Ireland's artery. *Waterways 3* explored the Barrow and the vein of Norman conquest. And by then waterways were beginning to look a little thin on the ground.

By a lucky coincidence, some years before, certain people of influence, including Charles J. Haughey, at the time head of government of the Republic of Ireland, had also been bitten by the waterways bug. They looked in particular at a derelict and unsuccessful navigation called the Ballinamore & Ballyconnell Canal, which the powers that were had set in train in the last century in the altruistic hope that it would provide relief to the famine-stricken peoples of north-west Ireland, drain some boggy land and provide a link between the waterways network of the north of Ireland and that of the south. It was a monumental failure. But in the early 1990s it was rebuilt by a talented engineering and design team from ESB International, just in time to provide a location for *Waterways 4*.

That brings us up to Chapter 1. It opens at the start of the fourth and probably the last, of my voyages of discovery along the inland waterways of Ireland. It is not just a journey through landscape. I travel with baggage – memories of a dead companion. May Dick Kearney rest in peace and may the contribution of his son give him a measure of immortality. And cultural baggage – I am a Southern Irish Republican Protestant … something of a paradox on two legs. This journey is from the south to the north and inevitably involves a reprise of too many centuries of tragic history. There's a war on here … or is there? Has there been an outbreak of peace? I want to know. And my interest is not just academic. I live here.

This is the background. What happened before this book starts. When I was asked to write it I was faced with an impossible deadline. Fifty-five thousand words had to be written in a couple of weeks so that the book could be published to coincide with the première of the television series. A very talented writer called Niall Fallon generously offered to help me out. The way we have divided up the work is that I have written a subjective essay describing my personal reactions to the people, places and events of the journey. He has written a series of objective and factual articles about the same things. What we hope we have achieved is to illuminate each item from three different perspectives – my subjective reaction, Niall's objective analysis and Mike O'Toole's wonderful photographic interpretations of the trip.

My wife, reading the transcript, says there's an awful lot of 'I' in it. She's right, as usual. All I can say in my defence is that I have tried to mitigate the egocentricity by being as honest as I can.

Because a television series and a book have been made about the same journey, and because both claim to be honest, it would be logical to expect them both to tell the same story. They don't. There are small differences in the route, the events and the characters. This is because, in order to be accurate and coherent, both media have to select from the actuality. They have to embroider and suppress in order to achieve an honest and stimulating impression of what happened, and each medium does it differently. A scientifically accurate log of day-to-day events would be no more honest, and would be less effective.

To put the whole thing in less abstract terms, consider what actually happens on a journey like this. It is being recorded for television on a single film camera. This requires that a mile of waterway may have to be traversed five times so the director can get different shots from different camera positions. Later she will, with the editor, create an amalgam, a composite, from five different journeys over the same mile. The book does the same, describes the same journey, but print requires a slightly different mix from celluloid.

Well, that's dealt the hand. Now it's time to play the cards.

Dick Warner

Dedication

Acknowledgements are boring and nobody reads them. But I would like to state that this book would not exist were it not for the absolute professionalism of everybody who has been involved in the production of the television programmes. No list of names – you know who you are and you know you're the best in the business. Thanks.

Chapter 1

The River Shannon, upstream from Carrick, is a familiar waterway. It sweeps northwards in broad loops, under a big sky. Then there is a fork. The Boyle River and Lough Key are to the left. I swing right, under Hartley Bridge, making for the headwaters. The river becomes narrower, lined by rushy meadows and purple loosestrife and placid cattle. I've been here many times before, heading for Leitrim village, or further up to Battlebridge and the canal to Acres Lake. But this journey is a little different.

First there is *Oxlip* – the boat I have borrowed for the trip. She's a steam launch, which is a new experience for me, and she is very beautiful. She gleams with varnish and polished brass. She also makes me a small bit nervous, as a new boat always does. Steam engines require rather more attention than internal combustion engines and all that varnish carries an implied warning … a bad scratch would have to be repaired by cutting back to the wood and applying ten new coats, each sanded wet and dry.

But the main difference about this trip, the main thing that fills me so full of anticipation, is the fact that Leitrim village is no longer a terminus. They have taken away that rather depressing sign which read 'End of Navigation'. Because the new Shannon–Erne link has opened and we're not at the end of anything, we're at the start of countless miles of cruising in new waters.

Declan knows this part of the Shannon too and I think he feels the same excitement and anticipation about the fact we're encountering something new. His father, Dick Kearney, was my companion, guide and tutor on the waterways for many years. He died some months ago and we're very conscious both of his absence and his presence. But Declan is, in many ways, another ideal boat companion. He's very competent. When something goes wrong, when we have one of those little emergencies which are part of every long trip in an unfamiliar boat, while I'm still thinking about what to do, Declan has done it. And already he's mastering the intricate details of the steam engine, which have me baffled. Also he doesn't talk much. He spends hour after hour in a sort of daydream, and so do I, and that's good. Sometimes, after an hour or two, his curiosity makes him break his silence … 'How old would that castle be, Dick?' … It's nearly always a historical question, and sometimes I know the answer. He has no objection to being incarcerated for long hours in pubs in the evenings, another point of compatibility, and sometimes, after many pints, he reveals the fact that he's a fine singer and tin whistle player. We get along fine.

The banks have come closer together and a magnificent white willow hangs out over the water. We cut in close to have a look and have to bow our heads beneath the hanging fronds. An occasional cruiser, plastic or steel, passes us, the crew looking a little puzzled at our shining mahogany hull, brass-bound boiler and long white smoke-stack. I'm impatient to get this over with, this known, familiar bit, and start on to the new waterway. We come to a blue sign, another parting of the ways. Left to Battlebridge, Acres Lake and, in the very near future, through another newly restored navigation to Lough Allen. We head to the right, into a canal cut, making for Leitrim village.

Leitrim village

When the village was a terminus it was a slightly depressing place. It always seemed to be raining on grey and shabby buildings and pot-holed streets. Old men in pubs stared at glasses of stout and thought about all their relations in America. But now there's a change. New jetties, of course, and lots of boats. But life in the pubs. Half a dozen nationalities chatting and joking and food being served and an upbeat atmosphere. And newly cobbled pavements with cast-iron street lighting leading up from a new harbour to the village. A public toilet block, which also has showers and a laundrette. And a man who's come to sell me smart cards. Smart cards?

Yes, the Shannon–Erne waterway, the politically correct title for the restored Ballinamore & Ballyconnell Canal, is a strange blend of the old and the new. I stand in front of a monument commemorating the heroic retreat of O'Sullivan Bere after his defeat at the Battle of Kinsale. A significant moment in history when the power of Gaelic Ireland was broken by the English. And the man sells me two cards for twenty pounds. They look like something you'd use in a card-phone or to get an emergency few quid out of the hole in the wall just before closing time. The same logo is on the card and on the man's sweater … a reef-knot joining two ropes, one orange and one green. It's a clever symbol for a waterway connecting Northern Ireland and the Republic. And the card? Well, I'm told it operates the locks … no balance beams and big cranks to wind up the racks here … and is also an open-sesame to the laundrette and the showers.

But the strange thing is that the overall impression is far from high-tech and new-fangled. A hundred and thirty years ago, when they were building the original waterway that failed, transporting heavy things was difficult and expensive. So they opened small quarries along the route and cut stone locally for the locks, bridges and quays. This gave the canal variety, as the colours and textures of the stone changed, mile by mile, and made it fit comfortably into its environment. Most of these stone structures were replaced by reinforced concrete during the restoration. But the engineers took down the old cut-stones, one by one, numbered them and stored them. Then they replaced them as a façade over the raw concrete and preserved some of the essential character and age of the waterway.

The first lock is only a few hundred yards outside the village. There's a nice comfortable wooden jetty just before we get to it so we can moor, careful of all that varnish, and hang lots of fenders to the gunwales and then walk up to look at the size of the problem. There's a stainless steel box on a plinth, like a one-legged robot, with a slot in the base for the smart card and lots of buttons and lights. There's also another man with an orange and green reef-knot on his chest to explain everything. Buttons to close gates and open gates and let water in and let water out and one marked EMERGENCY STOP. And a radio telephone link on which you can make a mayday call if the worst has come to the worst.

But it doesn't look too bad, really. We decide that Declan will work the boat and I'll work the buttons. And it all goes well. Under the watchful eye of the man with a reef-knot on his chest, we lock *Oxlip* up hill, through Lock 16, on the first stage of the climb over the watershed which divides the Shannon from the Erne.

Giraldus Cambrensis wrote a book in the twelfth century called *Topographia Hibernica*, which was a geography of Ireland and included maps. It was pretty basic but quite accurate, particularly about the courses of the major rivers in the country. There was only one odd mistake. He described the Shannon as a river with two mouths, one in Limerick and the other in Ballyshannon, and that's how it's shown on the map. He wasn't really wrong, of course, just a few centuries premature. The Shannon and the Erne actually rise within a few miles of each other but Ireland's largest river did not connect with her second largest river till the second part of the nineteenth century and, because that connection was so badly done, the journey we are going to attempt, from one river into the other, really only became possible in 1994.

Giraldus Cambrensis has another interesting bit in his book. He quotes a prophesy by Merlin that Ireland, a country of many nations, will one day be united.

There's another landing stage above the lock where I get back on board and take over the tiller again. I'm used to boats where I work the helm, the throttle and the gears myself. On *Oxlip* I steer and Declan opens and closes the steam valve to control our speed and performs some little conjuring act with rods behind the engine to change from ahead to astern. This requires a degree of communication between helmsman and engineer. At first there was a lot of talk. Not shouting, but 'A bit of reverse now, Declan,' expressed calmly but urgently as we approach a landfall. Already we are managing much more quietly. We have learned how much way our boat carries – she is over the ton with a fine entry – and can make the adjustments instinctively. We are getting confident.

It's a steep climb. The locks come one after another. At Kilclare there are three within a space of a couple of hundred yards (metres), and I call a halt. There's a ball-alley and a pub. I go into the pub … and learn all about the ball-alley.

The steam launch Oxlip

The information comes in pleasant, witty pub-chat from informed strangers. It reveals a down side to rural Ireland – the meanness and begrudgery and poverty. One priest preaching against another from the pulpit … about a ball alley … it all happened a generation ago, but it left a bad taste. Today County Leitrim is the most depopulated place in Western Europe, if you don't count the extreme north of Scandinavia. It's also one of the poorest. But there is a positive side. The very openness with which conversation is engaged and information exchanged, the palpable sense of hospitality to strangers … it evokes happy memories of my childhood when rural Ireland was a friendlier, more innocent place and when there were some compensations for poverty. This may be a little romantic – but I do like Kilclare.

The scenery's getting better too. Mountains are rearing up on both banks. Slieve Anierin, the Iron Mountain. It was probably given its significant name in the Iron Age. Sheebeg and Sheemore, the small and the big mountain of the fairies. And the title of a piece of music composed by Turlough O Carolan, the Irish Mozart, who spent some time in these parts. I once climbed Sheebeg with a friend on a fine day in early summer. He got to the cairn on the top and looked round at a magnificent panorama of hills, lakes and blossoming furze. 'You can see how a view like this must have inspired Carolan,' he enthused. 'Carolan was blind,' I pointed out.

Beneath the mountains, the canal threads its way uphill. We're nearly at the summit. A last lock and a dramatic cutting through limestone – small cliffs to port and starboard. And then the first lake.

The red and white half-moons of the Erne Navigation markers

Lough Scur is sudden and spectacular. Wooded islands, a dolmen on the shore, the ruins of Leitrim Gaol hanging out over the water. And a sign that we have reached a watershed. In the middle of the lake the familiar red and black markings of the Shannon Navigation change to the red and white half-moons of the Erne. We're getting somewhere now.

To celebrate we pull into the harbour at Keshcarrigan, a dangerous thing to do. Keshcarrigan has decided that the west's awake. There's a new harbour with a sign for the new restaurant and guesthouse and there's music going on in Des Foley's pub. We get sucked into a whirlpool. Keshcarrigan turns out to be an easy place to visit but a hard place to leave.

A hard place to leave: Gertie's in Keshcarrigan

When I eventually escape I turn *Oxlip*'s bow through a section of flooded river and into a pretty little round lake called Lough Marave. Treasure was found in this lake: a beautiful Bronze Age bowl called the Keshcarrigan Bowl, which is now in the National Museum in Dublin. Small golden water-lilies are in flower all around the shore and there are water birds everywhere.

It's getting late. The sun is sinking. We spent too long in Kesh. I push on at our best speed, through river sections and some lovely lakes with Canada geese on them. I need to find somewhere to spend the night.

Eventually we come to Kiltybardon Lake and pull up alongside a limestone peninsula that almost cuts the lake in half. It's a dream camping ground. There's water, fuel, shelter and a fine view. We set up lights, cook food, open bottles. Declan sings a song, which makes the sheep across the lake start bleating.

Eventually, very late in the night, I am left alone in my lonely campsite. The film crew and the boat drivers have all gone off to their guesthouse. Declan is sleeping on one of our support launches. I am on this long spit of rock with water on three sides of me and a canopy of hawthorn and ash over my head. The large campfire is dying back; occasionally a charred branch collapses and sends a column of sparks up to mix with the stars. I sit with a can of beer in my hand and my pipe between my teeth in front of the flaps of the brown canvas tent and I listen. There are still sheep bleating, there's the lap of little waves on the stones, a sleepy waterbird and a faint sound from the breeze in the leaves. A positive sense of peace settles on me. It's a palpable thing, like a blanket being wrapped around my shoulders. It feels very good indeed.

I smile at nothing in particular, wriggle backwards into the tent and fall totally asleep. *DW*

Tending to the boiler aboard Oxlip

The World of Steam

If ever any mode of transport could be said to typify a certain leisurely period in history, it would be the steam launch. Faded photographs of the Edwardian era, families boating on Lake Windermere in the English Lake District, crinolined ladies with prim hairdos and parasols to shade their complexions, straw boaters and striped blazers at university regattas – these are its images.

Why steam? Before the internal combustion engine came into being, steam was the principal means of mechanized transport the world over. Trains and ships ran on it; much of the power which drove the industrial revolution in the nineteenth century was provided by steam. It was inevitable therefore, that once its adaptability had been harnessed into areas other than industry, someone would decide to use it for leisure purposes.

This was easier said than done. It was one thing to use steam to drive a huge cargo ship or a train weighing many tons. It was entirely another to consider using it in a vessel say 20 to 30 feet (6–9 metres) long. For one thing, the machinery needed to provide steam was cumbersome – and still is. There's the boiler and the water tank and, not least, the engine to drive it all. And there is the fuel. All of this weighs a lot and takes up a lot of room – and as mariners know, there is always a shortage of room on board any boat, no matter how large.

The equipment needed for steam power also has other disadvantages. Any small vessel so heavily cargoed as a steam launch is close to being unseaworthy, one very good reason for confining her activities to inland waterways. In Victorian and Edwardian days, for instance, there were several fatal boating accidents on Lake Windermere involving steam launches which had capsized and sunk in windy days on the lake. With so much weight on board, a small vessel becomes unbalanced, unable to ride the waves; skilful seamanship is needed always and not least on lakes.

As well as that, anyone handling a steam launch must watch the weather and know when to set out on a voyage and more importantly, when not to.

For all of its disadvantages, steam launches have their dedicated followers who will not hear a word said against them. David Laing is one of them. An Englishman who studied at Trinity College in Dublin in the Sixties, he has been a steam buff since he was scarcely a teenager, and he has never lost that enthusiasm.

Oxlip, the boat which carried Dick Warner on the journey described in this book, is David's boat. How he acquired her – in a manner of speaking – is a long story. One day about thirty years ago he was attending a boat rally when he saw, nestled unobtrusively in the reeds, a perfect little steam launch. Entranced, he went to look at her. She was called *Oxbird* and had been built by an old man of eighty-one for use by a younger man – aged

David Laing, the owner of Oxlip

seventy-nine! – who had always owned a steamboat and, says David, 'wanted to die owning one'.

Later on in his life, David quite out of the blue met a man who said that he too was interested in steam launches and even owned one. That man was Derrick Mills, a famous name in steamboats, and the founding father of the Steamboat Association. And his boat? By the strangest of coincidences, she was none other than *Oxbird* – the boat which David Laing had seen hidden in the reeds years before.

As tends to happen to steam buffs, David had just one purpose in mind – he wanted his very own steamboat. But he had to make a living and other things intervened. Then one day he came to a decision; he would build his own steamboat. So he wrote to Derrick Mills to ask him if he could copy *Oxbird*. Certainly he could, was the welcome answer. And so began another steam odyssey.

David Laing and a boat-building friend from Co. Sligo, Rodney Lomax, went to see *Oxbird* and took some pictures and made some rough drawings of her shape and size. Later Rodney was to make the beautiful carvel hull from these drawings and his own sound memory – no mean feat.

What to build her from? They needed good mahogany. So they bought several cubes of the stuff in Belfast and sawed it up to make planks, turning them out a little thicker than the actual ones in *Oxbird*. By 1983, the hull was ready and waiting for the engine.

The engine. Now that was another problem. David Laing unearthed from Henley-on-Thames the name of a company which specialized in turning out a range of engines designed for modelling buffs. In 1914, David discovered, the firm of Stuart Turner had actually produced a prototype for a much bigger engine – and by another strange coincidence, that engine had ended up in *Oxbird*. New drawings and castings had been made, first shown at a Boat Show in the Seventies, of which a set was obtained. These were made up in Norwich.

That left the boiler, plus of course a few other little necessities. Bit by bit, the replica of *Oxbird* was being assembled, painstakingly and slowly but surely nonetheless. They got an engineer called Edward Langley to make the boiler, based on a 100-year-old type of which an original can be seen in the Science Museum in London. In the mid-eighties, after much effort, heart-searching and overcoming of many obstacles, the new *Oxbird* was born. David called her *Oxlip* – the name for the male flower of the cowslip.

In 1987 he drove from England to Ireland towing the 20-foot (6-metre) *Oxlip* behind to exhibit her at the Dublin Boat Show. Next door was perhaps the most famous steam launch in history – Humphrey Bogart's *African Queen*, from the famous movie of that name.

Like all steam launches, *Oxlip* is an eccentric little craft, needing plenty of humouring to get the best from her. She is an open launch – no shelter whatsoever when the wind and the rain get up. She's fuelled by what's known in the trade as 'steam coal', which is about half-way between house coal and anthracite. Unlike the image of engines puffing great billows of smoke, steam coal is actually quite clean and produces much less smoke and soot than other forms of fuel. But it's hard to get steam coal in these days of diesel and petrol engines, so when she's in Ireland – and all during her trip along the Erne waterway – *Oxlip* is fed splendidly on a diet of peat briquettes, the hardened blocks of milled peat culled from the almost limitless bogs of Ireland.

Running *Oxlip* smoothly is a delicate balancing act. It takes three-quarters of an hour for her to get up enough steam to start the day's work. First you check the water level, then you light a pile of sticks and a firelighter, put on a few briquettes of peat and wait for the pressure to build up. The engine and boiler are complicated by a mass of twisting and winding pipes which make them look like a Heath Robinson invention gone awry – over 120 boiler tubes have to be swept clean every day using a shotgun-cleaning brush.

And then there are duties like lubricating the engine and polishing her plentiful supply of brass. And of course two coats of varnish every year to keep her mahogany hull in sparkling order.

When she gets going, *Oxlip* runs surprisingly smoothly and quietly, one of the advantages of steam. Using about a bale of briquettes every hour, she can trot along at about 5 or 6 knots.

Oxlip was at home on the Erne waterway, redolent as it is with memories of other days. She slipped easily and effortlessly along through rivers, canals, lakes. At times temperamental – she likes her fuel dry and her pressure up – she became over those few weeks a fond home for Dick Warner through what proved a long and arduous journey.

The Making of a Waterway

'The navigation of the Shannon, if it were once vigorously and effectually carried on, and the cutting of a canal from Lough Erne to the seaport at Ballyshannon, would be two undertakings of vast advantage to our inland commerce, and indeed the last would be so feasible, and have such effects on that part of the kingdom, that it cannot long be overlooked …'

The words are prophetic. They were written in 1738 by the Reverend Samuel Madden in his robust *Reflections and Resolutions Proper for the Gentlemen of Ireland.*

Almost a century after the Reverend's wise words, the gentlemen of Ireland had got around to his way of thinking. Fuelled by the expansionary thinking of the day following the success of the industrial revolution, by the early part of the nineteenth century the Shannon had been made navigable from where it reached the sea at Limerick to its uppermost reaches in County Leitrim, connected to Dublin by canals and also connected, via the River Barrow, right down to the south coast at Waterford.

It was paralleled by its cousin in the north. Here Lough Neagh, the largest lake in these islands, was a hub of water which served as a link to Belfast, Newry and various other northern towns. The Ulster Canal actually connected Lough Erne to the Atlantic Ocean on the west.

But – again prophetically – there was no waterway which actually linked those northern and southern waterway systems, even though they passed within a scant 60 miles (96km) of each other. So in 1838, the Shannon Commissioners took the bull firmly by the horns and instructed a young engineer, William Mulvany, to survey a route linking the two systems.

Although Mulvany came back with a simple plan which envisaged a canal link across difficult and wet country, very prone to winter flooding, the many large local landowners along the route had their own ideas. They eventually persuaded the authorities that the building of the new waterway should be combined with a huge land drainage scheme and, in the light of this, a new plan was drawn up.

This would have three main sections. The Leitrim reach, connecting to the Shannon some miles above Carrick-on-Shannon, would convert the Leitrim River into a stillwater canal of about 3½ miles (5.6km) with a series of eight locks almost beside each other to enable boats to climb 80 feet (24 metres) in height as far as Lough Scur. The middle section, called the Summit reach, was an excavated canal from Lough Scur to Lough Marave, a stretch of about 4¾ miles (7.6km); and the final reach, called the Woodford Reach after the river which partly forms the boundaries between the Republic of Ireland and Northern Ireland, ran gently downhill through a series of eight locks for nearly 31½ miles (50km) to enter Upper Lough Erne near Belturbet in County Cavan. In between, the last reach called at such towns as Ballinamore in Leitrim and Ballyconnell in Cavan.

Work started on this ambitious project in 1846; and it was not the work of today, done by giant earthmoving machines and cranes. Men did it with pick and shovel and were usually recruited locally – a real bonus in a land where farming was often subsistence and people were generally quite poor. Gunpowder played its part in removing recalcitrant rock, and steam-dredgers were called in to excavate the channel across the lakes.

It was a time of famine and poverty in Ireland. The Great Famine of 1845–7, when the staple crop of the people, the potato, was destroyed by disease, killed millions of Irish people and forced millions more to emigrate. Thus the waterway construction came as a godsend to the locality through which it moved, foot by foot, for some years. At one time, 7,000 people were employed.

Irish waterways have a habit of coming unstuck in their making – the Royal and Grand Canals on the Shannon are a sobering example – and this latest one was no exception. Often work had to stop because there was not enough money to pay the workers' wages. But the main difficulty was that the original twin aims of the project, combining navigation with land drainage, simply did not gel.

There were other, even more serious, difficulties. By the time the canal was more or less finished in 1860, it had been outpaced by the growth of railways in Ireland – a similar fate befell the Royal and Grand Canals. And the canal itself was faulty. Lock chambers leaked, banks caved in, depths of water were too shallow. In 1869, just nine years after it had been opened, the waterway closed down. During those years it carried just eight boats – a total of less than one a year. And thus ended yet another woeful chapter in Irish canal history.

That chapter remained closed for 122 years. During that time, the waterway went its own way – or rather nature did. The physical structure crumbled quietly down the years; the wildlife grew apace, making the waterway one of the most unspoilt and prolific natural environments anywhere in Ireland.

Other forces were at work. Water-based tourism and leisure were growing rapidly. There were political reasons – the waterway served as a visible and symbolic link between two communities, North and South. The Irish and British governments got together and decided to re-open the waterway.

It was an ambitious and costly undertaking. Jointly sponsored by both governments, the £30 million project was carried out over three years by ESB International, who drew up the engineering plans. Money came from the European Union Regional Development Fund, the International Fund for Ireland and the ESB (Electricity Supply Board) in the Republic. The waterway is now looked after by the Office of Public Works from the Republic (it also looks after the Shannon Navigation and the southern canals) and the Northern Ireland Department of Agriculture, while cross-border cooperation is also evident in the marketing and promotion of the waterway, shared between the Irish Tourist Board and the Northern Ireland Tourist Board, with funds provided by the International Fund for

Reconstructing a lock on the old Ballinamore & Ballyconnell Canal

Ireland.

The work took three years and finished ahead of time and within budget. Basically the entire waterway was reconstructed to twentieth-century standards. It follows the old waterway exactly but there the resemblance ends. All the locks had to be re-built—under that old stonework there are precision-built shells of reinforced concrete. Bridges had to be raised or even replaced. The channel had to be widened and deepened to accommodate the bigger boats of today. All cuttings and embankments had to be remade. All vulnerable areas of bank and river-bed were reinforced with natural rock.

There were other changes which reflected the new era. The locks are opened by push-button technology, using smart cards and the mere touch of a twentieth-century finger. New moorings, ports, harbours and berthing spaces were provided all along the route, road access improved, new slipways provided, and a plentiful supply of tap water, car-parks, public telephones, showers, toilets, fuel facilities and so on put in place.

All of this inevitably caused severe disruption to the natural environment of the waterway, undisturbed for a century and a quarter. There was widespread concern that wildlife would be permanently harmed. The engineers thought of this too. The waterway was mostly excavated from one bank only; sometimes the machines actually crawled along the river-bed or were floated on pontoons to protect the fragile banks.

The work was done only during the summer and was scheduled to avoid disruption to spawning and nesting, flowering and migration. Fish were taken out and put into temporary quarters, later to be returned. Spawning beds were replaced and extended, fish-passes rebuilt, the waterway restocked. And the whole area on either side of the entire waterway was landscaped as naturally as possible.

Today the Shannon–Erne waterway stands as a monument to cooperation, progress and care for the environment. The Reverend Samuel Madden would have been proud of it.

Leitrim village: start of a new waterway

The Shannon–Erne Waterway: Some Facts

TOTAL DISTANCE: 62.5 kilometres, including 11.5 kilometres of lake, 42.5 kilometres of canalized river and 8.5 kilometres of stillwater canal.

CHANNEL: 1.55 metres deep, 13 metres wide at surface and 8 metres wide at the bottom.

LOCKS AND LIFTS: There are 16 locks, all push-button, electrically-powered and hydraulically operated. Each lock is 25 metres long and a minimum of 4.9 metres wide. They lift the waterway a height of some 45 metres from the Shannon and Upper Lough Erne.

BRIDGES: 31 road and access bridges cross the waterway.

VESSELS: The waterway will accommodate most river cruisers. Larger vessels are restricted to a length of 24 metres, a beam of 4.5 metres and a draught of 1.2 metres. Height from the waterline should be no more than 3.2 metres.

SPEED LIMIT: 5 kilometres per hour (3 mph) in canal stretches and harbour areas.

NAVIGATION: The channel is marked by perches, fixed stakes with a top-mark. There are two marking systems, the Erne markings applying to the stretch from the Erne through Woodford Reach to the mid-point of Summit Reach. Thereafter the Shannon marking system applies.

MOORINGS: There are six modern public moorings at Leitrim, Lough Scur near Keshcarrigan, Lough Garadice, Ballinamore, Ballyconnell and Aghalane. These are all equipped with slipway, car-park, telephone, toilets, showers, fresh water and pump-out facility. Other facilities are all the time being developed along the entire length of the waterway and there are plenty of other places to moor.

CRUISERS: Available for hire at Enniskillen, Belturbet, Ballinamore and Carrick-on-Shannon.

FOOD AND ACCOMMODATION: There are plenty of good bed-and-breakfast guesthouses, small hotels and good restaurants.

OTHER LEISURE FACILITIES: Golf, fishing, riding, trekking, walking, cycling, canoeing and many more.

O'Sullivan's March

On the face of it, the Irish clan of O'Sullivan seems an unlikely enough starting point for the creation of a military strategy which today is expounded at that most prestigious of military training academies, West Point in the United States.

The O'Sullivans were an old Gaelic clan who ruled in a remote part of the south-west of Munster, a territory which roughly covered the area between the Kenmare river in Kerry and Bantry Bay in County Cork. Towards the close of the sixteenth century, like other native clans, it had begun to feel the full effects of the colonization of the island of Ireland by Queen Elizabeth I of England. The O'Sullivans, like other clans in the south-west and also in the north-west, were among the last to be subdued.

At this time, Ireland's only realistic hope of throwing off the English shackles was Spain. In 1588, the abortive Spanish Armada, the invincible fleet of ships and men sent by King Philip II of Spain to invade and conquer Protestant England in the name of the Catholic faith, had been repulsed by a combination of bad planning, bad luck, bad weather and, not least, by the success of the English fleet in beating off the Spanish fleet and forcing it to head for home via the North Sea, Scotland and Ireland.

Many of the Armada ships were wrecked on the Irish coast, probably at least two dozen. At one time, there were at least 7,000 Spanish survivors gathered in the north-west, actually outnumbering the English troops stationed in Ireland and therefore, at least on paper, presenting a threat to English rule. However, that threat never amounted to anything and in a few months the Spaniards had gone and the threat with it.

However, neither the Irish nor the Spaniards gave up the struggle entirely. In Ulster, the great clan leader Hugh O'Neill still played out the last few games of his lengthy chess-like battle to deny England and to retain his own autonomy. O'Neill's shrewdness and ability to survive had spread its wings of encouragement throughout Ireland.

So strong had his influence become that in the last few years of the century, England had been forced to build up her troop strength in Ireland. In 1589, the gallant impetuous young Lord Essex, later to die in the Tower of London for his sins but a great favourite of Elizabeth, had suffered a humiliating military campaign disaster in Ireland, prompting his hasty withdrawal and the posting to Ireland of one of England's most senior, trusted and skilful military commanders, Lord Mountjoy.

The stage was now set for what was to prove the decisive confrontation in the long centuries of English–Irish conflict in the island.

Both O'Neill and Mountjoy were commanders and strategists of the highest order. Furthermore, O'Neill now had the open support of Spain, which landed a substantial force of Spanish soldiery in the Cork port of Kinsale in 1601. In one of the most famous battles in the history of Ireland – and certainly one of the most decisive, apart from the Battle of the Boyne in 1690 – the English, led by Lord Mountjoy, defeated the Spanish and Irish forces, led in part by the great Hugh O'Neill, at the Battle of Kinsale in 1601, marking the last efforts of Spain to win the long war it had begun with England in 1585 and marking also the last efforts of the native Irish clans to hold their own. Within a few years, the native chieftains had mostly fled the country. Their resistance was broken and Ireland entirely subdued for the very first time.

The O'Sullivan clan played a major part in the Battle of Kinsale. Before the battle, O'Sullivan had given his castle at Dunboy, a few miles away, to the Spaniards for their use. After the defeat at Kinsale, in which his own men had fought, he was told that the Spaniards were going to give up his castle to the victorious English. This was too much for him, so, gathering his men, he regained his own castle, prepared to fight to the last to hold it and, with it, the last vestiges of hope and honour left to him and his clan. But Dunboy Castle fell after just one day's savage fighting in which many English soldiers fell as well as Irish.

For O'Sullivan, who survived the siege in which he lost his castle, his lands and almost everything he possessed, the situation was a desperate one. He could not remain in Munster, as the province was being inexorably subdued by the English under their commander, George Carew. Despite intense diplomatic moves to get Spain to send further help to Ireland, he knew that this would not be coming. All that he could do was to take what was left of his small army, his clan and his family and try to make it to Ulster, where he could rely at least on the protection of Hugh O'Neill. And thus began one of the grimmest and most remarkable marches in Irish history.

O'Sullivan's task was almost impossible. He had to march some 200 miles (320km) across enemy-held territory, in which he knew that help would be practically negligible. He would be travelling in the depths of winter, when the weather was poor, and food from the land was difficult to get. Not only would he face the English forces but he would also have to face those Irish clans which had sworn loyalty to the English crown and could be counted on to oppose every step he took.

O'Sullivan took with him on this momentous march about 1,000 people – 400 soldiers and 600 other men, women and children. Going through Cork, he was attacked by the MacCarthys and afterwards by forces led by a brother of Lord Bantry. Both times, he suffered severe losses but kept on. He travelled doggedly through Limerick into Tipperary, where the county sheriff attacked him, again with severe losses.

His march northwards was then stopped by the banks of the River Shannon. With no boats with which to cross, O'Sullivan killed some of his horses and a boatmaker he had with him made some currachs, or hide-covered boats, using the skins of the horses they had killed. Once across the Shannon, they made their way as far as Aughrim in County

Galway – later the scene of a famous Jacobite–Williamite battle in 1691 – where they were attacked by the Burkes and O'Kellys. Surviving this, but with ever-increasing losses, they carried on to Ballinlough in County Roscommon, sniped at from all sides by enemies.

It was winter; the snow fell. They had little food and had no tents, having to sleep mostly in the open air. By the tens and twenties, people died each day, men, women and children. Finally, a full two weeks after he had left Cork, O'Sullivan reached the friendly castle of O'Rorke at Leitrim village, where the Erne Canal now passes through on its peaceful and quiet way north and south. Out of the thousand who had left Cork, eighteen soldiers, sixteen servants and one woman survived, as well as O'Sullivan himself.

The march of O'Sullivan Bere is remarkable for many things. It had the vision and desperation of a leader who had no other choice if he was to survive. He knew the dangers and did not underestimate them. Though he lost most of his force, he had fought a series of strategic retreat battles and skirmishes with consummate skill and courage against impossible conditions – superior enemy numbers, lack of equipment, food and shelter, the added burden of women and children who had to be fed, cared for and defended. Small wonder, therefore, that O'Sullivan's great and futile march towards an impossible dream has become the stuff of legend, inspiring a military generation many hundreds of years removed from its resourceful and courageous creator.

The Tale of Father Pat

As you edge your cruiser gently on to the quay wall beside Lock 10 on the canal at Kilclare in County Leitrim, you are almost in the shadow of P.J. Lynch's pub. A skip on to dry land, a few yards up the road and there you are – a haven of peace and pints and the gentle patronage of soft-spoken Peter – or P.J. as he prefers to be known.

The chances are that, if you're not from rural Ireland, you'll ask P.J. sooner or later about the squash court whose tall walls almost flank the walls of the Sheemore Lounge and Bar. And there you may betray your ignorance of the rural sporting Irish, for those walls belong not to a squash court but to a ball alley, wherein is played one of Ireland's oldest, most traditional and most neglected games, the sport of handball.

It goes back a long way. The legendary Irish hero-warrior, Finn MacCool, played it. It is a simple yet complex game of skill, speed and stamina. Think of it as squash played without rackets and you're close to the mark. Bare hands and closed fists are used to pummel a small, hard ball from wall to wall; and you'll know the handball expert by his bruised, battered and pumpkin-like hands. Hands that, unlike a squash racket bouncing off a side wall, take the full brunt of contact.

The chances are that, as you pass by the ball alley on your way back to the boat, you'll hear the sounds of play. Open the door and a few young men will be bounding about the court just as they have done in rural Ireland for countless years.

But it was not always so in Kilclare. The ball alley has a history – a history which in itself is a microcosm of social life in rural Ireland sixty years ago. Let P.J. Lynch take up the story …

It all started in the 1930s, a time of deprivation and bleakness in Irish life. The Republic was a new country fashioned from the difficulties of centuries. Standards of living were low, rural poverty high. Jobs were scarce and money too. There was little for young people to do in the country areas. Amid all of this, the Catholic Church ruled with an iron fist, its priests revered and respected almost as gods.

Into the quietness of Kilclare came a priest who had been for some years in Australia. Father Pat Ward, born in Leitrim and at the time of these events aged in his early sixties, had what might today be called a roving commission for his church. These days, with a scarcity of priests, there is always room for promotion to being a P.P. – a parish priest – but sixty years ago priests were in plentiful supply and often there was little enough work for them. So when they were semi-retired, they often came to rural parishes to help out the incumbent clergy.

Father Pat was an energetic man, with time on his hands. He had been a handball fan. Now he got together a bunch of local people and suggested building a handball alley. Local men chipped in with voluntary labour. Most of the materials were given free or begged, borrowed or even stolen. But while there was plenty of enthusiasm, there was no money, so Father Pat began a round of fund-raising activities – raffles, dances, all kinds of events. Once the walls of the alley were up, a local man lent a tarpaulin that normally covered hayricks and they put this over the four walls of the alley and held the dances there.

Dancing was, however, both a social and a religious problem. In the grey days of the thirties in rural Ireland, dancing was looked upon by the clergy in a less than favourable light, almost as the doings of the Devil himself. The stories of rural priests going about the by-roads late at night after dances and beating young lads and lasses out of the ditches is, alas, no joke. All dances were regarded suspiciously. So when Father Pat decided to extend his fund-raising activities by holding ceilis in the ball alley every Sunday to pay off the debt, it proved too much for the parish priest, Father Kiernan.

By this time, however, the ball alley was proving a wonderful boon. 'They were great days,' recalls P.J. Lynch. 'We all went there on a Sunday and danced for the afternoon. The dancing was from four o'clock until eight in the evening and the admission was two shillings and sixpence – a lot of money in 1933.'

Not just the dancing was popular – the real object of the exercise, the promotion of handball, also took off at a terrific pace as the young men came from all over Leitrim and neighbouring counties to play – from Boyle, Drumkieran, Dromod and even Carrick-on-Shannon. 'There were great players then,' says P.J. 'Men like Neddy Drum, Willie Earley, Leo Downes, John Golden … locals such as Jackie Forde and my own brother Sean. You

Handball as it is played today in Kilclare

The newly-opened waterway will open up a hidden area of Ireland which has been hard hit by emigration for many years

had to book your place on a weekend and in the evenings the game was so popular.'

But over it all hung the shadow of the parish priest, Father Kiernan. It was rumoured that he was objecting not just to the dancing and the frolics but also that Father Pat's fund-raising activities were affecting the amount of money which the parish itself would normally receive. So Father Kiernan took the then-unprecedented step of preaching from the pulpit at Sunday Mass against Father Pat and his activities.

The people, he thundered, should have nothing to do with Father Pat, should not go to his dances, should not even (and here was condemnation of a very serious kind indeed) go to his Masses. 'If you lie down with dogs, you get up with fleas,' trumpeted the parish priest.

In today's liberal and even anti-clerical climate, it seems incredible that not only should one priest attack another so publicly but the people should actually obey. And yet that is what they did. Such was the power of the rural clergy that the populace, afraid to risk Father Kiernan's wrath, stayed away from Father Pat, his Mass and especially the handball alley. Soon the dancing stopped. The players faded away from the alley. The frenzied weekend activity, when the sweating players yielded the court to the high-stepping dancers every Sunday afternoon, ceased altogether. Father Pat was sent to Sligo, where a few years afterwards he died.

During the Second World War, activity at the alley declined almost completely. As the years went on, other sports took precedence. TV and radio came. Few young men now ever opened the creaking door of the alley and belted a ball or scored a 'butt' down in the corner. But then in the mid-eighties, P.J. himself got a few locals together to form a committee and, with the help of government funding, restored the floor and the side and back walls with the help of such locals as Sean McKeon, Garda John O'Donoghue and Sergeant Carey from Carrick. Soon a roof will go on, making it all-weather; over three dozen good young local players are active and handball alleys are going up in other areas – Drumshanbo, Fenagh. A complete revival is on the way, a fitting memorial to the never-forgotten energy and drive of Father Pat Ward.

But there is a curious sequel. Father Pat was a man of many sides. One of those was his skill in faith-healing. People suffering from a wide range of illness and disease came to him from miles around, asking for his help; he listened, sent them away and then prayed for them. And, it is said, most of them recovered, leading to a firm belief that this priest was one who was more than usually gifted from God.

It's a belief which lingers on beyond the grave. For even today, the ill and the diseased make their way to Father Pat's grave in Kiltoghert and scrape off and take away the mould which grows on his gravestone in the belief that this man's ability to heal can reach out to them even from beyond the grave. It is as if the spirit and energy of this long-dead man of God still hovers in the quiet air of Kilclare, providing an impetus from beyond this life for the people to carry on the memory of a fine man.

A Man and his Music

In 1726, Turlough O Carolan, perhaps the best known of all Irish harpist-composers, wrote a poem of seven verses in which he praised himself to the skies.

Though the poem set out to be jesting and self-deprecating, like all jokes which turn on themselves, it was more truth than jest. In it, the harpist wrote of himself:

> *There is none like me in the race of Eve,*
> *It is not because I say so myself;*
> *By my oath I will tell no lie,*
> *My compeer shall never be seen.*
>
> *From me is each tale most melodious,*
> *It is I have been honoured by women,*
> *I am first in the power of the fingers,*
> *None like me will ever be found …*

O Carolan is one of the great Irish composers of the period, leaving behind a wealth of original tunes which to this day remain fresh and vigorous. He was also that peculiarity of the Irish society in which he and his forebear harpists had lived – a remnant of a courtly and kingly culture where the harpists were also bards, men who composed and sang lays and ballads about anything and everything. They were men who entertained king and commoner alike, who literally sang for their supper. In ancient Irish history right through medieval times and even up to O Carolan's time, they occupied a unique and singular place in the Ireland of their day.

Turlough O Carolan was born in County Meath in 1670 and died in 1738. Those sixty-eight years were to see apocalyptic events shake the very foundations of Ireland. O Carolan was in his early twenties when William of Orange defeated the exiled King James, thus re-establishing Protestantism as the dominant religious force in Ireland and copper-fastening a division of religion and culture in the north of Ireland which has remained to this day. They were events which were not lost upon the harpist as he played and composed his way around Ireland, for he spent much of his time in the Leitrim and Fermanagh areas – an area of land which was to become known as O Carolan's country.

By all accounts, O Carolan was an unusual man. A contemporary has written of him: 'Very few I have known … who had a more vigorous mind but a mind undisciplined through the defect or rather absence of cultivation. Absolutely the child of nature, he was governed by the indulgences, and at times the caprices, of that mother. His imagination, ever on the wing, was eccentric in his poetic flights; yet, as far as that faculty can be employed in the harmonic art, it was steady and collected. In the variety of his musical numbers, he knew how to make a selection and seldom was contented with mediocrity … gay by nature, and cheerful from habit, he was a pleasing member of society. And his talents and morality procured him esteem and friends everywhere.'

To understand O Carolan's world, it is necessary to know something of it. He was at his height during the repressive years of the Penal Code, imposed by an English-controlled parliament on Ireland. The Penal Code began in 1695, when O Carolan was twenty-five years old. It was directed against the practice of religion, education and the possession of property. Religion – the basic religion of the populace was a strong Catholicism – was a particular target; priests and bishops were forced to leave the country and could be executed for high treason if they returned. In many parts of the country, Mass could not be said at all. Being Irish, many bishops and priests refused to conform and there grew around the country a secret network of Mass-saying priests and Mass-going Catholics in defiance of the laws.

The penal code was equally draconian on the questions of education and land. Catholics could not maintain schools or colleges in Ireland; if they sent their children abroad to be educated as Catholics, they forfeited their lands and most of their few remaining civil rights.

As far as land was concerned, people were either made to become Protestants or were reduced by the complex laws to a state of beggary and penury. When a Catholic landowner died, his estate was divided among all his sons, unless one of them turned Protestant, in which case he was given all of it – a measure which effectively reduced the land-owning Catholic aristocracy to ruin in a few years. No Catholic could marry a Protestant and no Catholic could inherit from a Protestant.

The penal laws formed a central part of the society in which O Carolan moved and composed and they are central to the way he thought and lived. A particular target of his razor-like and satiric tongue was the many hundreds of families which had turned Protestant to save their lands and had adopted English rule and English ways – a U-turn encapsulated in the old Gaelic phrase '*an coirce do thabhairt ar an eorna*' – to give up the oats for the barley. The penal laws caused about 90 per cent of all the land of Ireland to pass into the ownership of people who were either planters or had adopted English ways and it also caused a mass exodus of young Irishmen to the continent, where they could at least make a life of their own in some sort of freedom.

In that area of Ireland in which O Carolan mostly lived out his life, the 'big house' was very much at the heart of so-called high society. The big houses were owned either by Protestants, by ancient Catholic families or by Catholics who had turned Protestant to hold on to their lands in the face of the penal laws. They formed a sort of oasis in the midst of a desert of deprivation; the landed gentry who lived in them had money and influence. They also had plenty of time and little enough to fill it with. It was, as one writer has put it, an age of high living and plain thinking, in which few of the gentry had ideas above a horse-race or a duel.

In this society moved the harpists. They would arrive at a big house and entertain the owner, his family and guests for a few days or sometimes even weeks and would then depart for another big house, where the process would be repeated. Thus they moved in a perpetual sort of circle, entertaining one big house after another and in between trying to make a living as best they could.

Very little is known of O Carolan's ancestry. Born in County Meath, his family moved to Leitrim and later to Ballyfarnon in County Roscommon, where the young teenager Turlough was to come under the favourable notice of the MacDermott Roe family, later to become his patrons. They owned an ironworks in the town which was fuelled by the ironstone worked in the neighbouring mountains of Slieve Anierin (literally the 'iron mountain') and others near Lough Allen.

When O Carolan was eighteen, he contracted smallpox and became blind. By that time he was showing considerable skill as a harpist and his patron, Mrs MacDermott Roe, placed him for tuition with another harpist for several years. Once he had completed this course, she gave him a horse, a guide and some money. At the age of twenty-one, he began his wandering career as an itinerant harpist.

Much of that life was spent in Roscommon, Leitrim, Longford, Cavan and Fermanagh, although there is evidence to show that he visited all the counties in Connacht, half of those in Leinster, one in Munster and two-thirds of the Ulster counties.

For four decades until he died at the age of sixty-eight, O Carolan pursued his life as a composer and entertainer with a steadfast dedication. There were milestones along the way: he married one of the Maguires of Fermanagh, and they settled near the village of Mohill in County Leitrim – if settled is the right word, since the harpist was perpetually on the road. They had seven children and Mary, his wife, died in 1733, just five years before O Carolan, an event he was characteristically to mark with a poem which ends:

I spent a space in Ireland happily and in content,
Drinking with every effective hero who was a lover of music;
When they had gone I was left solitary and sorrowful
At the end of my days, with my partner no longer alive.

O Carolan's mode of life was simple enough. He moved from county to county, from patron to patron. Mostly he would compose a poem, a lay, for his patron, often on a subject suggested by the patron himself. Moving from house to house along the muddy lanes of the west of Ireland, the blind harpist seated on a horse with his faithful guide carrying his harp, the journeyings must have been both demanding and romantic.

For O Carolan, the music came first – a musical historian has written that with him, 'O Carolan always made the tune first and the poetry last.' For all that he was indebted to the generosity and hospitality of patrons, O Carolan followed the ancient line of Irish harpists in that he was treated as a social equal by all those with whom he stayed. His sharp and satiric tongue was respected and even feared, and people were careful not to offend for fear they might become the subject of a biting poem which would mock them forever.

O Carolan died in the place where he had learned his profession as poet and harpist, the house at Alderford near Ballyfarnon where he had spent much of his young manhood. Thereafter began a bizarre saga which is still not resolved to this day. Many years after his death, O Carolan's body was uncovered and his skull removed. This was later hung by a ribbon in a church where the MacDermott Roe family, the earliest patrons of O Carolan, are buried. Later on it was removed from there and used for some strange rites, being used, according to one source, by some 'superstitious persons to boil milk in, which they considered cured many disorders, but more particularly the epilepsy'. The skull was also used in another way; epilepsy sufferers would scrape off portions of it, grind them and swallow them in a mixture as a cure.

Whatever the authenticity of the various skulls which have been claimed to be O Carolan's, another and more important relic lives on – his wonderful music, which is one of the greatest of Ireland's cultural treasures.

Chapter 2

I flash from complete sleep to complete wakefulness in one instant. There's a half-full can of beer, still upright, in my left fist. It's 5.45 in the morning. I feel as healthy as a wild animal. The odd thing is that I took my clothes off before I went to bed, though I can't remember doing it, and now it's cold, so I put them back on again.

The film crew is arriving. We are shooting 'dawn for dusk', picking up some low-light shots we missed the night before. The embers of the fire are still hot, so I boil a black kettle full of lake water for tea. I feel a slight sense of superiority. They all slept in beds. They are not quite as much a part of this as I am.

Eventually we get it all done, the tent is back in its bag in *Oxlip*'s bow and we have raised steam. We're on schedule, we're on the water and the travel thing is getting to me. I want to put miles under the keel, keep her moving, get to Ballinamore.

After the lakes we're on the Woodford River, though much of it is canalized and rather similar to the artificial waterway we took up the hill to the summit level in Lough Scur. I can make out the line of an old narrow-gauge railway along the port bank: the Cavan & Leitrim Light Railway, a favourite with steam buffs. If you're travelling in a steam launch you have to be, at least, a parvenu steam buff. And the railway has a long and intimate connection with the waterway.

The people who built the Ballinamore & Ballyconnell Canal, back in the last century, hoped that one of the main cargoes to be carried on it would be coal from the mines in Arigna. But they got the idea a little late, when the canal age was no longer in the first flush of youth. And it took them a very long time to build it. So, by the time it was finally opened to barges, the railway was there. And the railway took all the coal … and most of the other cargoes, and passengers too. As the railway prospered, and the waterway became down-wardly mobile, one began to encroach on the other. Canal company property on the quayside in Ballinamore was annexed for rolling stock and the new branch of capitalist transportation triumphed over the old. But in 1959 the railway closed and in 1994 the waterway reopened and even got back some of its quay in Ballinamore – so we won in the end. I give three hoots on the steam whistle as we pass the remains of an old rail bridge. My own little bit of triumphalism.

We stop at this quay in Ballinamore and television again intrudes on the journey. The director wants to shoot a sequence about the high-tech, card-operated shower units that have been installed here for boat users. The shower cubicles are quite small. I don't know if you've ever had the experience of being stark naked in a small shower cubicle with a cameraman wearing a fetching pair of pink trunks, a film camera in a bulky underwater housing, a smoke machine and a twenty-six-year-old female director? If not, you haven't missed much. I keep expecting to wake up from a bad dream. And the shower cubicle is so small that they have to wedge the door open to get the shots, and half the population of Ballinamore is peering in at the door, and the water is quite cold and there are a lot of takes, which means that what they're all peering at has shrunk to very unimpressive dimensions. The sound engineer is a motherly sort of man. He drapes a jacket over my goose-pimples between takes, and whips it off when the director calls 'Action'. Sometimes I think I should get a proper job.

It all comes to an end eventually. I dry off and get grumpily back into the boat. It takes half an hour of travelling to put me in good humour again.

It strikes me that I'm doing something that's unusual for somebody from the south of Ireland. I'm travelling towards the North. We don't really like the North, not for the past quarter of a century, anyway. I suppose it's not so much that we actively dislike it, as that it makes us uneasy. It's OK to read about it in the paper, see it on the news, discuss it in the pub; but to be actually confronted by the reality is embarrassing and unsettling … so most of the time we avoid the issue by staying down south. And when something forces us across the border we ask for advice about the route – maps are no good because the surveys they are based on don't take into account unapproved roads and blocked bridges. So we get directions to a road which has a British Army checkpoint and we sit in our car while teenage soldiers with bizarre camouflage and odd dialects from the regions of England ask us civil questions … and we don't know how to react. We start by resenting the Sassenach presence on the Holy Ground of Ireland … then we remember that the soldiers first arrived in response to Irish pleas for a force to protect the Nationalists from the Orangemen … then we remember that the Brits put the Orangemen there in the first place. Then we give up. It's much easier to stay at home.

And this sort of double-think is what makes the opening of the Shannon–Erne link such an extraordinary and significant event. It is a route that opens up the two parts of the island. It is a water connection across the divide. It traverses a part of the country where all the roads were closed – and many of the minds as well. It could be the first symbolic, faltering step towards that Ireland which has room for Catholic, Protestant and Dissenter. But, in the meantime, in the summer of 1994, it's drawing me closer and closer to the only war that's being actively waged in Western Europe. Which makes me just a little nervous. It's the first time I've ever travelled on a boat and wondered if this made me a target.

Then, lost in the daydream of river travel, I wonder what I will think if I take this book down from the shelf in twenty years' time, or stick the videotape of the television programme into the slot. It could be that this will become a strange little piece of archive, a diary from the last year of the war. And it could be otherwise. I'm interested in history, but I've never felt so much a part of it.

Lichens along the river bank

By evening I'm in an odd humour. I end up in a country restaurant: eating, drinking and talking. It gets late, but the company I have met say they were drinking with some people earlier in the day in a pub in Ballinamore and they promised to go back for a nightcap. Will I come? I may be old but at least I'm not sensible. Of course I'll come. We all pile into a Hiace van. We end up, six or eight of us, milling around the main street of Ballinamore about an hour and a half after closing time. Our leader is tapping on the window of a very closed-looking pub. I am filling my pipe under the light of a street lamp. Then I'm blinking up at the pub façade, and the lettering on it, which is all in Irish, in old script. At that moment the kitchen door beside the pub opens and a head, male, appears in the aperture and says: 'Don't you know there's a war on?' This chimes with my worst forebodings and I shrink into the shadows. But eventually our leader effects entry through the kitchen door and I slide after, the cowardly rearguard. I decide to say nothing. I have a problem – an accent which proclaims political views I don't necessarily agree with. And I have an intuition that I'm entering an establishment that takes politics seriously. For a while I say nothing, drinking whiskey with dedication and reverence. There are some strange people in this bar. Then one of them walks up to me sideways to make conversation. For some reason that's surreal, we talk about food. I expound on the pair of quail I ate in the restaurant earlier in the evening. He listens patiently, waiting for the opening. He's about sixty, quite small, quite ordinary really. Then he pounces. 'Did you ever eat horse meat?' 'I did,' I admit. 'I ate it in France and Belgium. It's not that bad.' 'It's great,' he says. 'Sure, I ate a piece of Shergar.' I am defeated. The night is too much for me. Time for bed.

It's a relief, the next morning, to return to the simple challenges of skippering a boat and the straightforward pleasures of nature.

I am impressed by the lichens along the river bank, particularly the ones on the trunks and branches of the trees. I have never seen lichens so lush and flourishing. I wish I knew more about them. I know that some species can live to be several hundred, possibly even several thousand, years old. I know that they have strange and marginal ways of feeding – dissolving nutrients from solid rock or distilling it from the air. And I know that they need very clean air. And this is probably why they flourish so well along here. The air is palpably clean and rather damp.

There is one image that contradicts the generally healthy nature of the landscape. The skeletons of dead wych elms dotted along the banks. They are, of course, victims of Dutch elm disease. But when I stop at Riversdale House, just outside Ballinamore, I get another environmental perspective on the elm tragedy. The owner of Riversdale heats the house by burning wood in a furnace. It's a very big house, a guesthouse, and it has a lot of

Riversdale House on the canal in County Cavan

outbuildings and half a dozen self-catering cottages and an indoor heated swimming-pool … and all heated by timber. And when I arrive he is feeding the off-cuts from some elm logs into the furnace. When I ask him what happened to the rest of the logs he takes me into a large conservatory with a very beautiful wooden table in it. It was made, apparently, by some Dutch furniture makers who are his next-door neighbours … out of elm which had died of the disease. The owner of Riversdale is English, the furniture makers are Dutch. There's quite a colony of people like this in North Leitrim. They are refugees from dirtier places who have fled to this part of the north-west to make their lives. They have brought with them many of the principles of the environment movement – including the idea of recycling things … even dead elm trees.

In the new weir below Riversdale there's a salmon pass. This is a fine act of faith, because there are no longer any salmon in the river. There were once, before the hydroelectric dam on the lower Erne disrupted the spawning run, but it is probably thirty or forty years since one's made it this far. The reason the engineers put a pass for migratory fish into the new weir is that the biologists believe that it may be possible to restore the run at some time in the future.

The sun is shining and I have a few hours of free time so I decide to go fishing myself. Not for salmon, not even for trout, which do still exist in the river, but for coarse fish. I tie *Oxlip* to a tree root and use a 5-metre pole with a small float and a single maggot on a size 16 hook, trotting the tackle down in the lazy current. The fish I most expect to catch is a roach. But actually I catch nothing, which puzzles me slightly, because I know I'm fishing quite well. I think the heavy engineering carried out in the course of restoring the waterway, which was combined with quite a lot of electro-fishing to move shoals out of danger, has disturbed the river too much. It may be next year or the year after before it's as good as it should be.

There's a maggot farm near here. Quite a big operation which supplies the whole of Ireland with bait, North and South, and does some export business. If you ever feel in need of a truly nauseating experience, go and visit a maggot farm. It's like a set for a horror movie with a smell added. The sight of a few thousand maggots worming in and out of the various orifices in a turkey carcass is bad enough … but there is also the fly house. A room containing a few hundred thousand large bluebottles which all fly at you when you open the door. And there's something else disturbing about a maggot farm. It's almost impossible to look at that turkey carcass without the thought occurring that, one day, this is going to be you.

I'm glad I don't believe in omens because the day seems to be full of them. The next macabre portent is a large leech which swims past my float with a peculiar pulsing motion. I give up fishing. I'm not getting anything, anyway.

The Ballinamore & Ballyconnell Canal was a rather silly name and I'm glad they've changed it to the Shannon–Erne Link. First of all there's far more river and lake on this waterway than canal. Second, Ballinamore and Ballyconnell are only two of the places it goes through, and neither of them is at the end of the route. The main difference between the two towns is that Ballinamore is in Leitrim, and in Connacht, and Ballyconnell is in Cavan, and in Ulster. This involves a subtle personality shift. I think about it for a while, and then decide not to. Racial stereotyping has done enough damage in this part of the world.

I decide to spend my free time sight-seeing rather than fishing and walk up the hill from the quay in Ballyconnell to visit the Protestant church. It's a very pretty church. Also, if you look closely, you notice that it was fortified at some time in the past. The time, of course, was in or around 1690. A Scots Catholic and a Dutch Protestant decided to fight a war in Ireland which was mostly about the succession to the English throne and Spain's designs on the Low Countries. History can get a little complicated sometimes. Anyway, James mobilized the Catholics of Ireland to fight for the noble cause and William did likewise with the Protestants. William won because he had more soldiers and they were better trained and equipped. God, once again, proved he was on the side of the big battalions. But the real losers were the Irish. Because the war planted the seeds of sectarianism which flourish in Irish soil up to today. They still paint 'Remember 1690' on walls in this part of the world. And they still remember it. And the same war is still being fought, 300 years on.

And the church? As far as I can gather the Protestant citizens of Ballyconnell got worried that James would arrive with his army and slaughter them, so they fortified their church and retreated into it with a small garrison. Rather pathetic, really.

Downstream from Ballyconnell the river forms the border between Cavan and Fermanagh – between the Republic of Ireland and Northern Ireland. The land gets flatter and the river starts to meander between wide horizons, punctuated by lines of willow trees. If William of Orange ever saw this landscape, he must have felt quite at home. It's like a little bit of foreign field that is forever Flanders. *Oxlip* is quite low in the water and, when the banks are high, there's not much of a view. But here I can see for miles … which is a very pleasant change.

Even pleasanter is a stop at Corraquill to visit Joan Bullock. She's a farmer's wife who is best known as a gardener. Her garden on the banks of the river is very remarkable. Unlike most gardeners she has a great love for nature and has created a skilful artefact which blends completely with its natural environment. You can't actually tell where the wild river bank ends and the garden begins. And bits of nature keep sticking their fingers into her handiwork – when I arrive she is good-humouredly replacing divots in a mossy lawn which a family of badgers have excavated the night before on an earthworm hunt.

She sits on a swing and we talk idly for hours about wildlife. I politely ask the names of some plants. She doesn't know them. This impresses me even more. Anyone who can

Part of Joan Bullock's natural garden on the Woodford River

make a garden which is as beautiful and as clever as this one and not even know the names of the plants she's doing it with is a real artist.

But there is one other thing that adds extra power to Joan's garden. It is bisected by an unapproved road and at the bottom of it there is a bridge which was blown up twenty-two years ago. Joan has lived here all her life and she tells me something I find very strange and important. Twenty-two years ago her neighbours 100 yards (metres) away on the other bank of the river spoke with the same accent she has. Now, since the bridge was blown, they speak with a Cavan accent on one bank and a Fermanagh accent on the other. *DW*

The damaged bridge at the bottom of Joan Bullock's garden. The Woodford River is seen through the remaining arch.

Branching into History

There's a verse in a song by the Irish comic writer Percy French which perfectly encapsulates the glorious uncertainties of the heyday of Ireland's small branch lines. It goes:

Kilkee! Oh, you'll never get near it!
You're in luck if the train brings you back,
For the permanent way is so queer, it
Spends most of its time off the track.
Uphill the ould engin' is climbin',
While the passengers push with a will;
You're in luck when you reach Ennistymon
For all the way home is downhill.

While there is a perhaps pardonable exaggeration in the verse, and in 'Are You Right There, Michael' as a whole, there is also something else – a deep fondness for the eccentric ways and humours of the little trains which once upon a time huffed and puffed their way uphill and down dale through some of the more remote parts of the island.

Alas, like those in many a country, Ireland's railways have fallen deeply foul of the modern mania for efficiency and cost-effectiveness. Apart from a starkly trimmed and minimal network of main lines, the branch lines have all gone, closing one after the other like a series of steel doors clanging shut from the twenties onwards. Today, the lines are buried by brambles, ploughed over, erased; they wander, neglected and forlorn, like forgotten children of another and more benign age. A few miles here and there have been restored but for all practical purposes, the intricate network which once spread like a cobweb right across the countryside is extinct.

Of course all of this has happened for a series of very good reasons. Rural Ireland, the backbone of the small branch lines, has been depopulating fast and for many years. The heavy industry essential to keep freight trains profitable simply has not been there in enough quantity to justify staying open. Agriculture, too, has changed and no longer are rural trains used as a way of transporting cattle and other farm animals, or indeed large quantities of grain. In many cases, much better roads and bigger trucks have eliminated the need for railways. Reduced more or less to depending upon declining freight carriage and fewer passengers, the writing was on the wall for the little railways from the end of the First World War.

In economic and business terms, it is of course true that the branch lines made no sense and therefore must be shut. But what has been ignored – and the point is a valid one – is that the closure of the branch lines has in itself contributed to rural decline. In the remote areas of the north-west, where the invidious motorway has not yet arrived, rural communities have in fact become more isolated; bereft of everything that a railway line brings with it – a link with the outside, an avenue of communications – these communities have suffered.

Two counties which have been particularly affected by rural decline are Leitrim and Cavan. Both are relatively remote from the capital, Dublin; both are essentially farming counties where the land is not among the best in the country. Large industries have been slow to establish there. The growth of tourism has been stifled by an under-developed road network. And then, of course, the counties have lost their railway.

The Cavan & Leitrim line was one of just three survivors of the narrow-gauge system which lasted, tremulously enough, right into the fifties, the tired remnants of a once-extensive network of lines which had criss-crossed the country. The narrow-gauge lines were built for cost-cutting reasons; being narrow-gauge they were both cheaper to build and to run, and were thus particularly suited to operating in the least populated parts of the country such as Cavan and Leitrim.

Ironically, the thinking behind putting so many narrow-gauge lines around Ireland was what would lead to their downfall. By their very nature, narrow-gauges could not carry as much as their heavier and bigger counterparts and between the two World Wars, and more particularly after the last World War had ended in 1945, road traffic began to eat away at the heart of the branch network.

The narrow gauges began to close, faster and faster. The first to go was the Portstewart Tramway in 1925; then two lines operating out of Cork city – the Blackrock & Passage and the Muskerry – shut down. Four of the engines used in those lines, by the way, were transferred to the Cavan & Leitrim line, where they had the unique record of having the largest driving wheels at 4½ feet on any Irish narrow-gauge line.

By the mid-fifties, just three narrow-gauge lines survived – the Clare lines (the subject of 'Are You Right There, Michael'), part of County Donegal and the Cavan & Leitrim.

The Cavan & Leitrim line had opened with some ballyhoo in 1887. It is unique in that from that year to the year it shut down in 1959, no diesel engine every desecrated its tracks. It was purely steam. People who have travelled on it remember with affection its diverse fleet of locos, all of them different, its end balcony coaches and of course its coal trucks. It remains one of the most photographed lines in Irish rail history.

The main line ran from Dromod in County Leitrim, between Rooskey and Carrick-on-Shannon, across to Belturbet in County Cavan, where it met another rail line. There was also a branch line – and a very important one – from the line's headquarters in the Leitrim town of Ballinamore to Arigna, the site of a huge coal mine.

It was this coal mine which kept the Cavan & Leitrim alive for so long when other narrow-gauges had long since collapsed. The coal quarried at Arigna was not of the best quality but there was plenty of it and it found a ready market. For many years most of it was carried on the branch line of the C. & L.; the branch line had been opened as early as 1888, only a year after the C. & L. itself had opened, and it was even extended in 1920 at a time when other narrow-gauge lines throughout Ireland were being looked at askance in economic terms.

The Arigna mine was central to the C. & L.; the locos even burned Arigna coal and in fact their large fireboxes were expressly designed for that purpose. The huge shipments of coal from the mine were transported to Belturbet, where they were transferred on to the Great Northern Railway trains by men with shovels – no heavy moving equipment in those days.

The Arigna line itself was a source of trepidation to anyone travelling in the area, for it followed more or less the road between Ballinamore and Arigna with little regard for the sort of territory it had to cross, or indeed any regard for any traffic it might meet on the way. At times it zig-zagged across the main road itself at ungated level crossings – a nightmare for any motorist coming on it without warning. But there were no real accidents.

The C. & L. lasted doggedly and well until 1959, when the duty of hauling the very last train on the Arigna line fell to Loco 2-6T No. 5. She chugged out of Arigna just after four o'clock on the evening of 31 March, filled with people anxious to have one last nostalgic journey on this relic of a bygone age.

Eltjo and the Elm

Eltjo van der Laan had always wanted a castle.

Castles, even in Holland, are scarce. And they cost a lot of money, more even than Eltjo, making a fine living as a master craftsman in fashioning objects from wood, could manage.

Besides, there was the quality of life in Holland. Too many people. Too much red tape. Too little variety in the scenery. Too constricting for the sort of man who likes to whizz around the countryside on a three-wheeled, exotically-coloured motorbike with scarlet and gold trappings. So Eltjo and his wife, Marion, decided to leave Holland and find somewhere more congenial to their life and temperament.

Eltjo van der Laan works on his elm furniture

They went all over Europe and could find nothing. Then they came to Ireland and decided, almost at once, that this was the place for them.

They looked at various houses. But there was little available which they liked and which was within the price range they had set themselves. Then they heard that properties in Leitrim were cheap, simply because it was remote and no one, it seemed, wanted to live there. To a young couple accustomed to the stifling over-crowding of Holland it sounded dreamlike. They came, saw Lawderdale near Ballinamore, and two hours later bought it.

It's a strange house, but typically Irish – or at least it used to be until the van der Laans got hold of it. Once it was a tower house, probably sixteenth century, and, as happens in Ireland, over the centuries people added bits and pieces. It finished up many years ago as a Georgian-style house, owned by local landlords, the Lawderdales, who gave to it their family name – Lawderdale House.

Today, under the hands of the van der Laans, the house is, well, arresting. They took the Georgian slate roof off ('it was falling down,' says Eltjo) and replaced it with one of painted galvanized iron. Eltjo's passion for castles appears all over the place in the form of castellated walls, decorative iron garden gates – and, not least, arising like a sentinel from the house itself, a tall square tower. And, yes, that tower has a galvanised roof.

Not that this would worry Eltjo. He's not a man to care for what anyone either thinks or says of him ('I hear the locals refer to me as that mad Dutchman who does nothing else but work his ass off'). He spends his time, as do his wife and son, making superbly wrought, hand-made wooden furniture, mostly from the sad remnants of Ireland's once-rich stock of elm trees, though other hardwoods like beech and ash are also used, increasingly so as the stock of available elm dies away. There is a sad irony in that a Dutchman should profit so handily from a disease, Dutch elm disease, which has more or less destroyed Ireland's elms but this does not diminish the quality of the furniture it yields.

Eltjo buys his timber more or less recently felled. It is then cut into thick planks and stacked carefully in an open shed, there to weather and cure for at least three or four years. Eltjo, far from trying to constrict his raw material into shapes which he can handle, likes the wood to cure in its own fashion and to its own wishes. Thus it will warp and twist, stay static, do as it will. Like a sculptor sensing the inner being of his material, Eltjo lets the wood speak for itself like a living thing.

The basic product is household furniture – chairs, tables. His chairs are sturdy, ready for several lifetimes' use. His tables vary from heavy, thick dining tables to naturalist coffee-tables, where the shape of the unhewn plank is allowed to wander at will. It all has something in common – a strength and individuality.

That's the way Eltjo likes it. His thriving business has grown not because of modern marketing and selling methods but because he relies on word of mouth to carry the gospel of his products. He doesn't go to shows, exhibitions, doesn't even have a catalogue. He merely makes things the way he wants to and when he gets tired of a certain pattern, no matter how successful, he discards it and invents another. He likes to talk to customers and listen to them but, in the end, 'With me, the customer is not king. If they don't like it, they can go to hell. I won't make things I don't like – it's that simple.'

Eltjo is sad about the demise of the elm but is philosophical about profiting from it. He will buy an elm trunk for between £60 and £70 and in four years' time may make some £4,000 worth of furniture from it. He does all the sawmilling, cutting and planing himself, as well as the design. His wife does all the staining and polishing, the neat finishing which adds a gloss to her husband's work. Son Waldo, with his own separate company, also contributes to the cabinet-making and follows his father's taste in three-wheeled motor-bikes.

Like many Dutch people, the van der Laans are environmentalists of a high order. They plant trees as fast as they use up those which others have planted long before them. Already they have planted over 30 acres of hardwoods and it is their ambition to have at least 300 planted within their lifetime. In this way, they hope to give back more to the Irish environment than they have taken away from it, however involuntarily.

Dead elm recycled into a beautiful piece of furniture

Bluebottles in Ballyconnell

'Bluebottles – now they're the lads,' says Barrie Nicholson with enthusiastic fervour. 'A big ,juicy fly will produce a big, juicy maggot. And that's what the fish wants.'

Not just the fish, it seems. At times of peak production in the summer months, Barrie Nicholson's Irish Angling Services can produce – wait for it – close on 40 million maggots a week for avid anglers coming to Ireland to fish for coarse fish, and even for trout.

Maggots, let it be said, are not measured by the thousand or even the million. Instead you buy them by the gallon or, more likely, by the pint. In case you really want to know, a pint of maggots is about 3,000 maggots. And when you bring them home to fish with them, you put them in the fridge for a day or two – slows down the metabolism and the frantic rate at which maggots want to become real, big, juicy flies, just like their dads.

Maggots are the favourite bait of coarse anglers, those dedicated and sturdy folk who spend their waking hours (within season, of course) catching and then putting back roach, rudd, bream, tench, carp and a few other species. Coarse fishing, as opposed to so-called game fishing, where the quarry is the lordly trout, salmon and sea trout (and also, for some reason, the grayling, which is absent from Ireland), is an immensely popular sport and growing more popular by the day. There are, it is said (who, one wonders, has got around to counting them?) well over 3 million coarse anglers in mainland Britain alone – that's almost equal to the entire population of the Republic of Ireland.

Ireland, says Barrie Nicholson, who runs Irish Angling Services, based in Enniskillen (the factory where the maggots are produced, however, is based in Ballyconnell in County Cavan, just a few miles down the road and across the border), is a great place for coarse fish.

He should know; he's been here for close on a quarter of a century. He used to run a bakery in his native Nottinghamshire ('Had a company car, expenses, all the usual things') and in his spare time went a-fishing. It was fishing which brought him to Ireland, one among an annual lemming-like migration of men who came to Ireland for the fishing, particularly when the close season operates in mainland Britain from spring to early summer (there is no such season in the Republic).

It was always men who came; women were a rarity. 'Men would go on an annual holiday with the missus and kids, say to Blackpool or maybe to Spain,' explains Barrie. 'But it was usual to keep aside a week or so to go to Ireland just to fish, fish and fish.'

One of the main difficulties which anglers faced when entering Ireland from abroad and then spending a week or so fishing was the lack of live bait. At first many brought over their own, but maggots are perishable creatures and soon change into bluebottles if given even the slightest chance. An angler, if he was lucky, might get a couple of days fishing with maggots brought over from England to Ireland; after that, he resorted to the normal bait used by every self-respecting Irishman, a good juicy worm.

Barrie Nicholson is an angler but he is also a businessman and he recognized that here was an opening – supplying live bait to English and other anglers coming to fish in Ireland. He used to send a van over to the UK and bring back a vanload of maggots and casters (an advanced version of the maggot). Gradually, visiting and home anglers came to look to Barrie to supply them with maggots. He saw that the business could and must grow, so back he went to Nottinghamshire to pick the brains of local bait farms there, gathering facts and figures of the esoteric business of breeding and selling maggots.

Within a few years, Irish Angling Services was up and running. Today, with a fleet of four vehicles and with Barrie's two sons running the Ballyconnell operation, maggots wing their way to every corner of Ireland. The firm is the largest maggot factory in the entire country and the only one, says Barrie, with a regular and countrywide delivery service.

Breeding maggots is a little more complex than Barrie's breezy definition of 'big, juicy fly equals big, juicy maggot'. The trick, he says, is to know in advance just how many maggots you need to produce to keep the market satisfied at any given time.

In theory, the essence of breeding maggots is simple. You take a bluebottle, the bigger and juicier the better. It matures after about a week, lays its eggs (preferably on meat) and dies a week later. In reality, the process is a delicately balanced one which has to be monitored vigilantly all of the time, whether production is large or small. The flies – and there could be anything from 20,000 to 40,000 of them buzzing around their own part of the factory, called a fly-house – live in a constant temperature of about 18 degrees Celsius. Fed on a rich mixture of demerara sugar, water and fish (they show a marked preference for minced cod), they mature within a week and then lay their eggs on a bed of fish flesh laid out specially for the purpose. These are continually removed from the fly-house and within twenty-four hours have hatched into tiny maggots.

These beds of maggots are then split into smaller beds, each holding say between 30 and 40 gallons of maggots, which are fed richly on a diet of soft meat such as fish or minced poultry for two days. Then, like an infant child, their feeding is upped to include more solid turkey and chicken meat, sometimes twice a day if required. Maggots feed for only six days and then stop – full stop. They will not eat again, ever, but for those six days they eat voraciously for twenty-four hours a day, and only on fresh food (the myth about maggots thriving on rotten and putrid flesh, says Barrie, is without any foundation).

At the end of this you have, as Barrie says, 'a pure-bred, 100 per cent bluebottle maggot'. Somehow he manages to make it sound as if he's just bred a Derby winner.

If all of this sounds ticklish enough, making sure the maggot arrives in tackle shops and other distribution centres in good order – and remains that way for some days – is even trickier. Maggots turn rapidly to the next development stage of their short lives on the way to becoming a bluebottle. This stage is called a caster, and casters are, it seems, just as effective a bait as the younger maggot stage. But even all the tricks in the world will not stop a caster from going on to the next vital stage, when the whole reproductive process begins again. 'You can delay it for a time but you won't stop nature,' says Barrie Nicholson.

At the end of this chain of production – or at least the human end – is the angler. All he wants are good, fresh maggots – and yes, they have to be big and juicy. Making certain that these are always available to every angler who wants them on a countrywide basis is a logistical nightmare, but Barrie Nicholson views it as one of the most vital cogs in his business machine.

'You've got to know more or less precisely how many maggots you need to satisfy your customers from one end of the week to another. We work on a pre-order system through the tour angling operators, who are paid commission as an incentive for all orders received. We get them to tell us how many anglers will be here at a given time, what they want in the line of bait, and then we make sure that the bait is there. We will guarantee that every order we get will be fulfilled. And because we work so closely with the tour operators, particularly in mainland Britain, we often know more about visiting angler numbers than even the Tourist Board!'

The peak months are May, June and September, with the mid-summer months of July and August only 'modest'. In winter, production can fall right back to maybe 10 per cent of its peak.

Irish Angling Services is a surprising success story – surprising because it is in a business area whose potential has not always been recognized. For Barrie Nicholson and his wife, living and working in Ireland has been just as much of a success. His two sons, Andrew and Peter, who were just five and seven when the family came to live in Ireland in 1971, are now married to local girls and are very much involved in running the business.

In all that time, this quintessential Englishman has never had an anti-English remark aimed at him and speaks highly of the help he and his family have received all through the years when he was building up his business. In their own odd way, the big, juicy maggots of the big, juicy bluebottles may have done more for the cause of ultimate peace in the island of Ireland than many a bigger and better-known venture.

The Story of 1690

The story of the year 1690 is in essence the story of the island of Ireland for the last five centuries. The principal event during that year, the Battle of the Boyne on 12 July, is powerfully symbolic not merely because of the battle itself but because of what it signified; and it had then, and has still, the most profound effects on the history of Ireland.

As with so many aspects of Irish history, that of 1690 is a complex one. It has been represented as the victory of Protestantism over Catholicism, of England over Ireland, of colonialism and empire-building over democracy, of might over right – and indeed of much more. In fact, it was an amalgam, a complicated mix, of all those factors and a few more besides. But an understanding of the issues which came to a head at the momentous Battle of the Boyne is necessary in order to understand also the problems of the relationship between Northern Ireland and the Republic.

In the sixteenth century, under Elizabeth I of England, there began the strongest effort yet by any English monarch to subdue and colonize the entire island. Ireland had been claimed by England when King Henry II came there in 1171 with the imprimatur of an infamous Papal Bull issued by Pope Adrian IV (the only Englishman ever to become Pope). Adrian had empowered Henry to take over Ireland with such encouraging words as 'You desire to enter the island of Ireland to subject that people to laws and to root out therefrom the weeds of vice … we deem it pleasing and acceptable that you should enter that island and execute whatever shall be conducive to the honour of God and the salvation of that land.'

A Protestant church in the Irish countryside

In fact, for several hundred years afterwards, England made only spasmodic and ineffectual efforts to colonize and conquer Ireland, which until well into the sixteenth century remained feudal, Gaelic and Catholic. It was only when Elizabeth came to power that a sustained and serious attempt began to change all that.

While the entire island came under English subjection much more than it had ever done, the province of Ulster posed particular problems. It was a province of contradictions, being at once the most Gaelic and the most settled. The bulk of the foreigners who came to settle the lands of Ulster under the protecting arm of Elizabeth were Scots Protestants, who were given huge tracts of land throughout the province, much of which was properly owned by the great native Irish clans such as the O'Neills, O'Donnells and Maguires.

The inevitable conflicts created by the imposition of a form of Protestant colonialism on a Catholic native clan system have been perfectly encapsulated by an Irish historian, who wrote of the sixteenth century: 'Ireland represented an almost classic case of the new problems posed for governments by the clash of competing creeds ... although Irish society was infinitely less sophisticated than that of the Netherlands, its struggle against English domination was characterised by the same features as the Dutch struggle against the domination of Spain. In both societies a religious cause enhanced, and was enhanced by, a sense of national identity. In both, the affiliation of national leaders to an international religious movement provided new opportunities for securing international assistance.'

Thus the seeds for what happened in 1690 were, by the end of Elizabeth's reign at the turn of the sixteenth century, well and truly sown.

Close on a century later, what has become known as the war of the two kings brought the situation to a conclusive clash. In 1685 the devout Catholic King James II succeeded his brother Charles on the English throne – an event greeted with joy by Irish Catholics and with trepidation by Irish Protestants. Catholics hoped that James would restore Catholicism and the native Irish to their rightful places: Protestants hoped that the status quo would prevail. Protestants were of course in a minority throughout the country, though they were more numerous in the north. As a historian has said: 'Protestants feared, and Catholics hoped for, a reversal of government policy that would affect civil and military employment, religion and the ownership of land.'

In essence, James did set about restoring the position of Catholics in Ireland, though not without immense problems; he was after all, an English colonial monarch with a domination over Ireland which was bitterly resented by many of the old Gaelic clans. His position was a difficult one: when he died, he would be succeeded by his Protestant daughter Mary, which would mean a reassertion of Protestantism in Ireland – definitely not to be accepted by Catholics. The birth of a son to James's second wife in 1688, however, altered things

King Billy remembered on 12 July, the anniversary of the Battle of the Boyne in 1690

again, with a prospect of a Catholic dynasty – definitely not acceptable to Protestants.

In the meantime, in the late 1680s, the Protestant William of Orange, a rival claimant to the English throne because of intermarriage between the royal houses of the Netherlands and England, had begun actively to undermine James. A complicated series of events led to James leaving the throne and fleeing to France, to be replaced by William, now William III of England.

As ever in the affairs of Europe, France was to play an important part in the events which followed. King Louis XIV had declared war on the Dutch in 1688 and when the exiled

James sought help from him after he fled to France, the French king realized that supporting the Jacobite (James's) cause in Ireland was a useful way to bring even more pressure to bear on William, who now had to fight on two fronts, in continental Europe and in Ireland. So in 1689 James landed in County Cork, accompanied by a party of Frenchmen. The idea was that, together, the two would raise an Irish army, defeat William and restore power to James.

James was welcomed back to Dublin with open arms. He then set up a parliament which was a disaster. The many opposing views and rights – of Williamites, Jacobites, Irish and English – which James had to reconcile through his actions were impossible for him to handle. He tried to recoup lost prestige by besieging Protestant Derry, but after a famous siege of 105 days his forces gave up the siege. Thus did James sustain a severe blow and the Williamites a great boost.

By the spring of 1690, William decided that he would have to come over to Ireland himself and deal with James on the ground, as it were. He arrived in Belfast in June with a fleet of 3,000 ships and 15,000 men and almost immediately marched south to meet James. The two forces came face to face across the broad waters of the River Boyne near Drogheda on 12 July.

That day is full of symbols, but there was one whose reverberations are still felt. William's 36,000-strong force was composed of Dutch, Huguenots, Germans, Danes, English and Ulster colonists – all Protestants. James's force of 25,000 troops were Irish and French – all Catholic.

The battle was minor and over very quickly. William sent his right wing to cross the river upstream, drawing James' strength away from the Oldbridge fords. Presuming that the battle was going to be upstream, James moved most of his army there, only to find that the two sides could not get at each other across an impregnable marsh. In the meantime, down at the ford, Williamite forces crossed and in a flanking movement easily defeated the third of James's army which had been left there. The Jacobites retired in disorder; three days later, James fled to France.

The Battle of the Boyne was the trigger that set off a series of events which resulted in the total defeat of the native Irish and were to set the tone of the divisions which beset Ireland today. Once more, Ulster in particular became a Protestant stronghold, linked like a limpet to England. The events of this century, which saw an Irish rebellion, a treaty with England which created in effect two countries, one with six counties, the other with twenty-six, and a civil war between Irishmen for and against that treaty and division, are a direct result and reflection of the events of 1690 and afterwards. Thus the very mention of 1690 brings to every Irish person, north and south, two sets of images. It is those images, and the bitternesses, hatreds and prejudices which they arouse, which have created and sustained the sad division of the island.

A Wild Garden

If one wanted to pick one place which more than any other typified the contradictions and the dichotomies which are part and parcel of the delicate relationship of Northern Ireland and the Republic, it would be Joan Bullock's garden on the Woodford River.

The river divides North and South. Outside Joan's thatched eighteenth-century farmhouse home the road runs by, southwards towards the Cavan village of Belturbet. But you can't cross the river at the end of the garden because, in 1973, paramilitaries blew up the bridge.

Joan remembers that night well. She and her family, with two young children, were tucked in bed when the knock came to the door. A few minutes' warning was all they got, time enough for them hastily to don some warm clothes and run away up the road away from the bridge before the bomb went off. Pieces of rock from the sturdy stone bridge whizzed over the farm, damaging buildings, trees, shrubs, livestock …

Life went on. The authorities came and restored the bridge with a span of iron. Soon another knock came to the door on another night; there was less time, and more damage. To this day the gap remains in the bridge, with the brown waters of the Woodford River sliding past downriver to the spanking new mooring point where hire cruisers delicately tread the imaginary line in midriver which divides people, religion and culture.

Joan Bullock's house on the border of Northern Ireland and the Republic

It is an irony in itself that in that quarter of a century which Joan has spent in her husband's old family farm, twenty-five years in which unimaginable cruelty and division have hit the community, her garden should grow quietly, undisturbed and serene, an oasis of tranquil peace in a riven land. This is no ordinary garden, however, for Joan Bullock, a woman whose social conscience drives her to work closely with a cross-community group in bringing peace to the area and to such works as bringing daily lunch to a ninety-three-year-old man living on his own nearby, is a woman who believes in and practises the natural way of gardening.

To the average gardener, this is hardly a garden at all. True, there is a neat rectangle of grass in front of the charming cottage, with its dangling roses and herb beds. But elsewhere there are beds of nettles and ferns, wild raspberry canes, a wandering and dense profusion of indigenous trees and shrubs through which meander trodden paths closed in on all sides by vegetation. There are areas over which Joan runs the lawnmower but even that, one feels, is done reluctantly; this is a garden not for people only but for the whole of nature, meant for, besides mankind, the birds, the bees, the butterflies, the beasts.

When Joan married into the farm, her husband's people had already created a garden. Her husband's grandfather, she thinks, must have been a gardener on the big estate owned by Lord Erne, a few miles away. He had been trained at Kew Gardens in London and brought with him to Fermanagh some fashionable tastes in trees – wellingtonias, cedars – which form a towering backdrop to what Joan has added. There are magnificent poplars which line the banks of the river, Scots pine, maples, ancient hawthorns, apple, ash, willow. Everywhere there are buddleias, placed there specially for butterflies – there are plenty of red admirals and peacocks.

Sustaining and encouraging wildlife is one of Joan Bullock's principal concerns. Despite the fact that there are cats everywhere – black, white, tabby and a mixture of all three – birds nest at incredibly unsafe low heights, almost as if their trust in this woman outweighs their fear of the feline dangers. A kingfisher flashes through the gap in the river bridge, its shrill whistle like a sound-dart travelling fast. Herons steal frogs from the pond the family have dug in the hollow where the river used to run, over which hover iridescently beautiful damselflies and dragonflies. There used to be a pair of dippers, lovers of fast, fresh water, but they have not been seen for some time. Spotted flycatchers nest under the edge of the thatch, whitethroats dodge about in the secret recesses of the thickets, blue, coal and great tits feed busily in the insect-rich vegetation.

It is not only birds that thrive in this wild place. An otter searches the river for his favourite food, the eel, and sometimes brings his family to the feast as well. The resident badger is a bit of a nuisance, nosing large holes in the ground as he slug-hunts at night; there are hedgehogs, hares, mink. The mink are a danger to the wildfowl eggs; they scare the geese and ducks, which come honking fearfully into the farmyard when they see or scent them.

Gunnera growing in Joan Bullock's garden

And then there are the wild plants, the natural decorations of nature which sit so uneasily in the urban garden – hogweeds, cow parsley, wood anemones, fungi, nettles. Down by the river, a strange and eerie path treads a way through giant growths of Japanese knotweed – a bit like a broad-leaved bamboo. Royal and hart's-tongue fern grow in secluded and dank places.

Through it all there runs something like a theme of triumph. This quiet woman, working unceasingly for her community, in which she herself clearly sees no division, no bitterness, has created an enviable memorial to her own cause.

A Man of Wales

Although the Irish have rich pastures, good fishing and hunting, but poorly developed agriculture, they have 'little use for the money-making of towns'; they are a lazy people who think that 'the greatest pleasure is not to work and the greatest wealth is to enjoy liberty ...'

The words are not those of some twentieth-century travel writer doing a 10,000 word article for *Time*. They were written by a man called Giraldus Cambrensis, otherwise Gerald of Wales, a Welshman of royal birth who came to Ireland in 1183 when Ireland had just been conquered by the Normans and who later on, in the true manner of the observer who knows there will be no comeback from those people whom he criticizes, took a long, slow swipe at Ireland and the Irish in a book called *Topographia Hibernica*.

Giraldus undoubtedly was a man of opinion – and, if the truth be told, his description of the Irish as a race who preferred liberty to wealth is still largely accurate. But he was not always accurate; he thought that the River Shannon, the longest river either in Ireland or in mainland Britain, actually had two mouths, of which the upper one debouched at Ballyshannon in Donegal. (Incidentally, Ballyshannon's name probably has nothing to do with the River Shannon either topographically or indeed in language; its Gaelic name is Beal Atha Seanaidh, or the mouth of the ford of the slope. Shannon itself means ancient goddess, an appropriate name for a mighty river like the Shannon.)

Giraldus called the Shannon the 'Sinenus'. 'It rightly holds the chief place among all the rivers of Ireland, whether old or new, both on account of its magnificent size, its long meanderings and its abundance of fish. It rises in a certain large and beautiful lake but divides Connacht and Ulster and sends two arms, so to speak, in opposite directions of the world. One arm goes south, flows beside Killaloe, takes in Limerick and, separating the two Munsters from one another for a distance of 100 miles (160km), pours itself into the Brendanician Sea ...

The other arm, of equal importance, separates Meath and the further parts of Ulster from Connacht and, after many wanderings, eventually joins the Northern Sea. It therefore separates the fourth and western part of the island from the other three. It runs between them and marks Connacht off from sea to sea ...'

So much for the accuracy of Gerald, man of Wales. But he was keen enough on Ireland to come back two years after his first visit in 1183 and begin some thorough research for his later book. Remember that he was judging Ireland in the light of the invading force of Normans, a disciplined, military people who built strong castles of stone and had an excellent political and financial administration.

The Normans were an expansionary and colonial people; the Irish were not. Thus there was little incentive for the Irish to work hard. An eighth-century manuscript, the Crith Gablach, describes the average week of an Irish chieftain or small king as consisting of two days of public business with the rest devoted entirely to sport and pleasure such as deer-hunting and chess. Farming was non-scientific and consisted mostly of grazing herds of animals. The commoner farmers, who held land under a chieftain, are described as men of some substance, having a house, a herd of cows, oxen, bulls, sheep, pigs, boars and a horse. His farmhouse was well supplied with the needs of the day – malt, salt, charcoal, bacon, milk, ale. He did not work hard because he did not have to.

Wherever he went in Ireland, Giraldus bent a disapproving and biased eye. Everything was viewed through the eye of a man to whom nothing that was Irish could be any good whatsoever. Of the Synod of Cashel, at which a set of religious strictures were imposed on the Irish people by King Henry II of England, who first 'took' Ireland in 1177, and which were designed to 'enlarge the bounds of the Church, to teach the truth of Christian faith to the ignorant and rude, and to extirpate the roots of vice from the field of the the Lord', Giraldus wrote approvingly: 'Indeed both the realm and church of Ireland are indebted to this mighty king for whatever they enjoy of the blessings of peace and the growth of religion; as before his coming to Ireland all sorts of wickedness had prevailed among this people for a long series of years, which now, by his authority and care of administration, are abolished.' This of a land which had been known throughout the civilized world for its learning and was called the Island of Saints and Scholars!

For all that, he was a man of principle. Years afterwards, he was to remind Henry's successor, his son King John, that his father had not kept his pledge to keep the Irish on the straight and narrow path of religion nor had he (the king) looked after the structure or organised religion as he had promised to do.

'The poor clergy in the island are reduced to beggary; the cathedral churches, which were richly endowed with broad lands by the piety of the faithful in olden times now echo with lamentations for the loss of their possessions, of which they have been robbed by these men and others who came over with them or after them; so that to uphold the Church is turned into spoiling and robbing it.'

The writings of Gerald of Wales, whether or not they are accurate, have lent a fascinating and angled insight into the Norman invasion of Ireland, an invasion which was to transform the country. Contemporary accounts give us much detail of the military aspect of that invasion but Giraldus is unique in that he travelled the country as an observer in a high position, allowed to go where he wished and with the time and disposition to delve into matters which soldiers and colonial administrators might well ignore.

Because of this, and also because of his discursive, lecturing and righteous tone, he cast an enlightening eye on Ireland and the Irish which gives us a clear picture of an age whose social structure and mores might otherwise never have been so chronicled.

Leeches and Legends

It goes under many different guises. None of them are easy to get a tongue around. There's *Helobdella stagnalis* and *Boreobdella verrucata*, for instance; and *Theromyzon tessulatum* and *Glossiphonia heteroclita*. And *Trocheta subviridis* and *Haemopis Sanguisuga* …

To most of us, it's simpler to call it the leech.

The leech arouses strange divisions of emotions in people. Either you like them or you are repulsed by them. The former category is in a very definite, even tiny, minority. For most of us, the leech induces shuddering revulsion.

And yet the leech is both an entirely harmless and most useful creature. The popular public vision, culled from B-movies and mainstream science fiction, is of dense and fetid jungles infested with parasitic monster leeches that suck the very blood from unfortunate human victims. Like most urban legends, that of the leech as a bloodthirsty monster is very wide of the mark indeed.

So what exactly is a leech? It's a small, wormlike creature with a sucker at either end, which lives in water (there is one species in these islands which is amphibious, by the way). Leeches live by sucking the body fluids, not necessarily blood, from other animals, but in these islands there is just a single species which is big enough and strong enough to pierce human skin and suck blood – the medicinal leech, otherwise known as *Hirudo medicinalis*.

Hirudo also has another distinction – it's the biggest of the leeches found in Europe by quite a long way. Most leeches are quite small, about an inch or so, but *Hirudo* is a big chap, going up to about 90mm or some 3½ inches long. Not by any means the sort of creature you would wish to find in your bath water …

The leech's suckers are perhaps the most interesting part of it. There's a small one at the head and a much bigger one at the rear and the leech uses them in two ways – one for moving itself along, the other for the less attractive process of attaching itself to its prey and gorging on its body fluids.

Basically, leeches are divided into two types – one with a proboscis, the other with jaws. The latter category is by far the smaller; there are just three leeches in these islands which have jaws, including *Hirudo*. This species feeds on blood – real blood – from all sorts of mammals, frogs, toads and fish. And people if it can get them. The other two with jaws include the horse leech, which belies its name by feeding on worms and snails, which it actually swallows, while the third of the jawed species is actually not a bloodsucker at all but eats insects and small crustacea.

The other lot have varied ways of living. Some are fish parasites, attaching themselves to the fins and cloacal regions; some are parasites of the slow-moving and thus easily catchable water snail. One greedy one, *Theromyzon tessulatum*, is fond of water fowl and lives by sucking blood from the wall of the nose or mouth.

Of all the leeches known to man, the medicinal leech, *Hirudo*, is quite easily the most famous – or even infamous in popular mythology. *Hirudo* was used for hundreds of years not just in folk medicine but as a serious and scientific way of treating illness and disease. Large quantities used to be imported into Ireland at one time, when the use of leeches in medicine was popular. Attached to the human skin, which it can pierce with its strong jaws, *Hirudo* was used for blood-letting, principally to relieve such illnesses as blood pressure; for most of us, the thought is a repugnant one—but if you live in Ireland, you can relax. *Hirudo*, it seems, does not dwell in the country, according to most sources.

There is, however, plenty of evidence that *Hirudo* was once a part of Irish wildlife, albeit in an indirect way. Whether it ever bred here seems at best problematic. There are records of it in such places as Lough Mask in County Mayo, from Blarney in County Cork and also from County Dublin, but modern research has tended to regard such records with suspicion, believing that either the wrong species has been recorded or the specimens were actually imports and not natives.

There is no doubt that *Hirudo* was widely used in Ireland for blood-letting purposes, being imported in large quantities; probably it was stored at times in natural water, such as ponds, and it could certainly have spread from these. Recent surveys, however, have failed signally to unearth any specimens from anywhere in the country. Most of the medicinal leeches were, it seems, brought into Ireland from Wales, but none seem to have survived the passage of years.

Add to this is the question mark which has been placed by modern Irish researchers over the validity of previous records of *Hirudo* and the picture seems even clearer; you need not fear, when travelling the Erne waterway, that a bloodthirsty specimen of *Hirudo* is going to fasten itself to your thigh and start his evening meal …

If however, *Hirudo* is absent, there are plenty of other species present in Ireland – about fifteen in all. The biggest of these is our friend the horse leech, otherwise known as *Haemopis sanguisuga*. He's about 60mm long, or some 2½ inches – not quite the monster that *Hirudo* is, but big enough for nervous eyes. But *Haemopis*, thankfully, is not a blood-sucker, surviving by eating worms and snails and other small creatures.

Haemopis also has another distinction – it is the only amphibious leech in these islands. It is also very widely distributed and is plentiful in the Erne basin, and if you don't want to see it alive and eating, there's a specimen in the National Museum in Dublin which came from around Belfast. *Haemopis* is easy to find – just look under stones, decaying vegetation and in the soil at the water's edge, or in the water itself.

All in all, Ireland's leeches are harmless creatures pursuing a quiet life of their own. Together, they well and truly squash the legend of blood-sucking monsters; after all, a creature just 2½ inches long can't do that much harm. Or can it?

Chapter 3

The navigation is becoming quite complicated. The Woodford River, which has been floating *Oxlip* along the damaged border between Cavan and Fermanagh, is joined by two other rivers – the River Finn and the Erne itself. The chart is like a blue web spun by a mad spider – an interlace of lakes, channels, ponds and streams. The dark blue is navigable water, the pale blue potential shipwreck.

This is temptation. I can't resist the idea of diversion, of exploring off the route, changing the journey from the linear to the lateral. So I check the chart again, swing the tiller impulsively and head to starboard, making for Foley's Cut.

In less than a mile – one small lake and a dredged channel – we pop out on to a large river. Foley's Cut is a short cut linking the Woodford River to the Erne. The Erne at last. A strong river flowing out of the Cavan drumlins, headed for the sea. I let its current catch the keel and take us with it. Round a couple of bends, past a shallow lagoon where swans are conferencing, and another turn to starboard at the junction with the River Finn. We've spent less than a quarter of an hour travelling on the Erne, but we'll be back. I'm just going to take a little trip up to the Quivvy Waters … because I like the name.

There are a few cows, masticating absent-mindedly and paddling through the shallows, a dab-chick diving under lily pads and a big, cloudy sky. Very little sign of human activity. No other boats. The channel narrows, and then expands into a little lake. There's a plantation of conifers on one shore and the scenery has a Canadian look. I feel like a voyageur, exploring eighteenth-century Ontario in a long canoe. Will there be Pince-Nez, with beaver skins for barter round the next bend? The water's shallow and the bow is pushing through a sea of emergent vegetation. I close the steam valve and take a sounding with the boat hook. We're still OK, there's a couple of feet between our keel and the fertile mud. Bubbles of farty gas rise up where the boathook has penetrated. Half steam ahead, and we press slowly up this headwater.

What a forgotten wilderness. Plants grasping at the varnished hull, climbing up the banks in carboniferous clumps of reedmace and sedge, flower gardens of loosestrife and marsh marigold, giving way to fields of furze and groves of goat willow. The birdlife is just as rich. The nasal mutterings of mallard and coot, waterhens and mute swans, great and little grebes and honking, atavistic herons. It's the sort of place where an unconfident person could begin to feel a little irrelevant. It belongs to nature.

And then something very strange rears up slowly behind a low ridge, dead ahead. At first I can't make out what it is, even with the binoculars. And then it dawns on me. Here's humanity's contribution to this lost landscape. It's a tower, two towers, resembling the look-out towers round a maximum security prison. Here, at the top of the Quivvy Waters, at the Limit of Navigation sign on the Finn River, is a British Army checkpoint on the road between the Republic and the North. The road is just behind the ridge and can't be seen. But as I inch forward at half speed in *Oxlip* the tops of the towers are revealed as two sinister eyes watching the countryside.

Once upon a time the Ulster Canal joined the Finn River around here and the waterway continued through Lough Neagh to Belfast. But nowadays this is the end of the line. I have to turn *Oxlip* and, stern pointed at the watching towers, head back down the Quivvy Waters. But I don't have to retrace our route for long. This part of the waterway is full of choices and there's a course that takes us under Galloon Bridge towards Crom and the start of Upper Lough Erne and our journey to the sea.

Ireland boasted a breed of landlord with an eye for the picturesque: Rockingham Estate on Lough Key, Muckross Demesne on the lakes of Killarney, Crom Estate at the top of Upper Lough Erne. They prospected for the finest land and waterscapes on the island and then they bought them – or maybe they annexed them … I don't know – anyway, they ended up owning large skelps of the most beautiful parts of a beautiful country.

Cows graze peacefully by the water

Crom is a little different, though. The gents with double-barrelled names no longer live in Rockingham or Muckross. But the Earl of Erne still makes his home in Crom Castle. He doesn't encourage shabby water travellers to drop in unexpectedly for a cup of tea and a chat – which is fair enough. But that will not prevent *Oxlip* from tying up at a jetty to explore the estate. This is because all the estate, apart from the 'new' castle and its gardens, have been handed over to the National Trust, who manage it so as to ensure that the public has access and nature is conserved.

Crom Castle from across the water

There is an old castle too, at Crom. A picturesque ruin on the shore. A little too picturesque, because some nineteenth-century Earl with more enthusiasm than taste decided to add on some fake bits to stir the romantic sensibilities lurking beneath the crinolines of a young lady of the county. But, if the ruins are a little thin on credibility, two trees redeem the situation.

I walk across the lawn to a great, dark green mound of vegetation. I'm interested in trees. They're one of my main hobbies. So I've read about the Crom yews. But nothing has prepared me for this, this thing, this extraordinary mount of verdure. I walk into it. I'm in a space between two very old and very strange trees. Dozens of dark red branches twist like the tentacles of sea creatures and twine together, forming a roof slated with dark green needles, under which I stand and worship.

Religious belief before Christianity is one of the least well-preserved aspects of our past. One thing we do know is that Irish pagans worshipped nature, in various manifestations, and that yew trees were very important in that liturgy. The primeval forest which covered this island was a dense, difficult and dangerous place. If you stumbled through it, 3,000 years ago, you might have come upon a big, old yew tree. The yew was the only large evergreen in the forest – holly and juniper were insignificant and pines were banished to the mountain – and yew forms a very dense canopy for twelve months of the year. So, in the deep shade of this canopy, was a clearing – a place where nothing else grew because there wasn't enough light. And this clearing, maybe 30 yards (metres) across with the bole of the tree in the middle, was the obvious place for the clan to meet – to discuss things, feast, arrange marriages … and worship. And one of the objects of worship was the great evergreen tree itself – symbol of the cycle of life, of the fact that children are born just as old people die, that winter is followed by spring.

This is the power of the old religion and this is what I felt when I walked into the yew cathedral of Crom.

One of the ancient yews of Crom Wildlife Park, open to the public

Outside the cathedral is an interpretative plaque that tells lies. It lies, in particular, about the age of trees. These yews are very old and very magic. They are older than the Earls of Erne, older than the Maguires and the O'Neills, half as old as time. They are probably the two oldest living things in Ireland. That's yet another reason why we should worship them. As I get older I become increasingly convinced that age should be venerated.

The county Fermanagh is full of big houses and Crom Castle is not the only one which should be on the itinerary of pilgrimage for yew-worshippers. In the relatively recent past, around 1740 to be exact, the estate at Florence Court had a talented and observant young gardener called George Willis who, while climbing a nearby mountain called Cuilcagh, spotted two seedling yews growing in a grove of junipers which were unlike anything he'd ever seen before. They were upright, erect and slender. He transplanted one to the garden of his own cottage and gave the other to his boss, Viscount Mount Florence, for planting in the Florence Court Demesne. News spread, and cuttings from the trees were given to friends. Botanists became interested and declared the tree a new species, *Taxus hibernica*. Other botanists disagreed (it's a habit they have), and today the tree is regarded as a sport, mutant or form and its Latin name is *Taxus baccata* f. *fastigiata* … in English, the Irish yew. It has spread all over the world and it's hard to find a cemetery, formal garden or public park without a couple of them. In Fermanagh they're even planted, rather incongruously, in cottage gardens.

But to get back to George Willis, the Viscount and the two original seedlings. It seems George's tree did well but the Viscount's died within a few years. The Irish yew can only be propagated by cloning, by taking cuttings, and all are female. So all the Irish yews in all the world are clones of one original, George's surviving tree. And survive it does, at a very healthy 250 years of age. And you can go and look at it if you want. I did.

I visit other big houses as well. Castle Coole is on the outskirts of Enniskillen. I think someone told me that they've just spent £7 million on its preservation. This is because it's such a perfect example of the Palladian mansion. They don't let me inside the front door, but I prowl around a bit outside. A great, big limestone lump set in a lawn with large, well-maintained trees growing out of it at mathematical intervals. Georgian architecture is highly fashionable 200 years later. It's based on the Aristotelian notion that the cube is a perfect shape. Maybe it's Euclid, not Aristotle. Anyway, this notion appeals to people educated in very old-fashioned and expensive schools where Euclid and Aristotle are still on the syllabus. But look at this house – it's ugly. And nowhere on it, around it, or within 200 yards (metres) of it, is a single flowering plant. It's like an old book in a library which nobody reads. I don't like it.

My dislike, when I probe it, is ideological as well as aesthetic. There's some sort of socialist reflex there which is worried by such an ostentatious display of wealth in a countryside so full of poverty. And it's not just the money they had … have. It's the privilege. They are the empowered ones in a land full of frustrations. Marie Antoinette would have felt quite at home here.

Better to be back in the boat, where our external combustion engine pushes us gently through a scattering of wooded islands. It's a beautiful evening, with a pastel sky sitting like velvet on the calm surface of the lake. What is the weirdest sound in all the world? If you are travelling across a lake in Northern Ireland on a still evening, full of significance, and you hear a peacock's scream across the water – that is the weirdest sound in all the world.

The sound comes from Inis Rath, an island dome of trees with a clearing in the middle with a large house in it. Feeling a bit like Ulysses, I am drawn towards it.

At the jetty there's a landing craft. These boats were originally designed to put tanks on to beaches during invasions. Now they're popular with islanders who use them as ferries. This one has, painted in large and fading letters down each side, the words HARE KRISHNA. I walk ashore, up a straight avenue cut in the woods, past peacocks, to the house – a large Victorian villa in need of some paint and glazing. The Hare Krishnas are living here '*en famille*'. Husbands, wives and children, and a few single people, mostly men of fifty or sixty. They seem to have come from several different countries, mostly English-speaking. There are English accents, American, one Indian, Irish, North and South, and a New Zealander. They are all wearing Indian clothing, to some degree or another. A few are authentic, others just drape a cotton dhoti over shirt and trousers. They smile a lot and are very hospitable. The hospitality is of a puritan nature. A drink is out of the question, and no smoking on the island. No meat either, and they don't like swearing. They run a Hindu school for the children, but most of the time is spent in liturgy. This consists of a service of singing and dancing which lasts up to an hour and is performed five to seven times a day. I am given delicious vegetarian food and invited to stay the night. I accept … and slip out into the night for an illicit smoke.

I get up just before dawn to take part in the sunrise service, the most important of the day. We file, sleepy-eyed, into a bourgeois drawing-room in the process of redecoration. There is practically no furniture, and an alcove at one end, curtained off like a small stage. Women stand on one side of the room, facing the stage, men on the other. Some have very small brass cymbals in their fingers. The master of ceremonies enters. He is a wiry man of indeterminate age with a slight English accent and a very confident manner. His head is shaven and he is wearing pale pink robes and some make-up and carrying a sort of bongo drum. He greets me pleasantly and I mutter something apologetic about the fact that I don't really know what I'm doing, but I'd like to join in, if he doesn't mind. He doesn't mind.

The music starts, a slow rhythm of percussion and chanting. Most of the chanting is in a language I don't understand, but occasionally I recognize bits of English. The curtains are drawn and reveal a most glittering, gaudy, colourful altar, with figures, half life-size, of a man and a woman in ornate Mogul dress and a young child in something that's a cross between a cradle and a swing. And the rhythm gets a little faster. And we're dancing, shuffling, shifting weight from one foot to another. And things are going on up at the altar, people are taking it in turns to hold a ribbon which swings the baby in the cradle, but the rhythm is getting still faster and the man in pink is getting quite intense and there's a film of sweat in my eyes and I'm losing track a little of what's happening. These people must be so fit!

Things calm down then. Dishes of flower petals are offered round by a child. Everyone takes a few and walks over, genuflects, and places them in a little silver dish in front of a holy statue of someone or other. I watch carefully, and then add my few petals.

And the rhythm hots up again and faster and faster. And then it gets unbearable. The noise and the colour and the speed of the rhythm and the necessity, the absolute necessity, to keep time with the dancing. And I realize that something quite strange is stealing over me. They don't need tobacco or alcohol on this island. This ritual is drug enough. I'm getting high, my mind is floating off, doing strange things. And as for the guy in the pink, he's on another planet. He's transported by what he's doing. We're all in deep narcosis.

But it feels great when you come down. No hangover, just a feeling that you've taken a lot of physical exercise and experienced something rather pleasant. I understand the attraction of it all … and I'm rather sorry that I have to leave, to walk back down the hill, past the peacocks, and untie my boat and head on down the lake.

It strikes me that this landscape breeds religion. In the past few nano-centuries of history there's been a spot of bother between the Catholics and the Protestants. But before that there were the monks, Culdees and Anchorites, drawn to the islands by a magnetic force. And before that? Celts and pre-Celts, searching for yew shade and island sanctuary. A spiritual tradition that stretches, unbroken and unchanged, over several millennia cannot be entirely without a basis. There must be something here. The Hare Krishnas must be right.

A large trout, not a vegetarian, rolls in the surface beside *Oxlip*'s port quarter and engulfs a daddy-long-legs, blown by the breeze off the holy island of Inis Rath. *DW*

Ireland is a land of green and grass

Forty Shades of Green

If you think that Ireland is a country covered by grass, consider this … The world contains over 10,000 different species of grasses, of which only about 150 or so are found in Ireland.

'Contrasting our grass flora with those of other areas similar in size,' one grass expert wrote dispiritedly of these islands, 'one is impressed by its poverty both in numbers of species and in its representation of the main groups of grasses …'

The very look of Ireland, filled with fields of grass, roads lined with grass verges, verdant lawns ranged neatly in suburban rows, gives one instant impression – that this indeed is a land of green and of grass. But not nearly so much as it should be, for Ireland has a climate which is eminently suited to grass-growing and whose promise it has not lived up to.

Why is this? The relative paucity of species has been explained in various ways but there is some agreement that our grasslands are the way they are because of the glacial activity to which Ireland has been subjected, along with its isolation from the bigger land masses, such as Africa, where the grass is much more diverse.

There is, too, the factor of a changing and much-changed landscape. As farmers have grown more efficient, tillage has got greater, grassland is lusher but less varied, marginal land is being absorbed into mainstream farming.

All of this has had far-reaching effects on the sort of plants which the land can support. Many species of flowering plants and associated fauna are threatened by a wide variety of dangers – direct habitat destruction through farming activity for one. Plants which are acutely sensitive to any changes whatsoever in their environment are most at risk. A case in point is the cowslip, one of the loveliest flowers in the wild. Cowslips thrive on well-drained and limy soils, but today you will not find them in efficiently farmed fields, where silage production and pastoral farming, with the consequent hazards of constant ploughing and re-seeding, not to mention herbicides and fertilizers, have produced a monotonous green sward whereon little thrives except certain grasses. What chance for the delicate cowslip amid all this progress? Small wonder that it has been declared a protected species in Northern Ireland …

Modern farming has indeed much to be responsible for. Once plentiful, and now becoming rarer, are such plants as carline thistle, salad burnet, kidney vetch, marjoram, corn marigolds, field roundwort, wild pansy, green-winged orchids, yellow mountain pansy … the list goes on.

Luckily enough, a great deal of the land which surrounds the Shannon–Erne waterway has escaped much of the depredations which have had such a stealthily secretive effect on Ireland's flora. Lough Erne and its convoluted islands and shores in particular help to support many species which have become either rare or localized in these islands in recent years.

There is a great deal of fen grassland, a wet and acidic environment, as well as other environments which together help to support such species as purple moor-grass, marsh pea, marsh stitchwort, gipsywort, skullcap, needle spike rush, trifid burr marigold, yellow loosestrife, meadowsweet, marsh cinquefoil, purple loosestrife, great tussock sedge, yellow iris, floating sweet grass, great willowherb, angelica and many more.

Being a land of almost as much water as land, the waters in the area are rich in aquatic plants as well and together form one of the most important habitats in the country for a variety of aquatic, emergent and swamp vegetation. Lough Erne's waters are by no means the cleanest and clearest in pollution terms: most of the waters are polluted in some way, primarily through too much agricultural fertilizer seeping from the land into the many water sources. Thus many of the loughs, for instance, have a regular algal bloom.

Land and water merge along the way

However, in the midst of all this, aquatic plants thrive. There is plenty of Canadian pondweed, spiked water milfoil, the ubiquitous chara, pondweed, three species of duckweed, including the quaintly named fat duckweed. Emergent plants you will see both in swampland and near the water's edge include the cowbane, greater water parsnip, flowering rush, tussock sedge, water soldier, and arrowhead, while you will also see less prevalent plants such as the lesser water plantain and reed sweet grass.

The woodlands too are rich in flora. Expect to see such species as liverwort, bird's nest orchid, wood sanicle, goldilocks buttercup, pignut, pendulous sedge, thin spiked wood sedge and so on.

The area is also rich in lichens, that mysterious growth of which we appear to know so little. Lough Erne's woodlands, particularly in Crom, are nationally important sites for lichens. Here a variety of mature trees in open parkland and shaded woodland have provided what are ideal habitats for lichens to thrive, about fifty species of them in all. Some of them can be read by foresters and tree-experts as indicators that ancient woodland was once common here.

Much study remains to be done on the flora of the waterway but one thing is certain; a variety of factors – geographical and political isolation, a prevalence of water, the presence of large estates and woodlands, relatively unchanged farming practices and so on – have helped to preserve and even enhance the area's rich stocks of grasses and plants.

Flowering rush: the waterway is rich in grass varieties

An Animal Kingdom

Every now and then in the salerooms and auction houses of these islands there surface, begrimed with the dust of ages and often decidedly moth-eaten, the impressively wide and fierce antlers of what many people call the Great Irish elk.

Impressive it is. The antlers can be as wide as 10 or even 12 feet (3–3.5 metres). The size of the bony and skeletal head, from which all flesh and hair have long since vanished down the ages, is intimidating. This was a big animal.

But the legend, like most legends, is only partially true. The Great Irish elk is not an elk at all, but a deer. A big deer admittedly but indubitably, a deer.

In many ways, the story of the elk which is not an elk is typical of the wild animals of Ireland. Although England, Scotland and Wales are just a few miles away – the nearest distance between them is only fourteen miles or so, between County Antrim and Scotland – Ireland has surprisingly few species of wild animal, many less than its near neighbours. We have, for instance, no dormice, harvest mice, moles, wild cats, roe deer and weasels. And we have only one shrew.

There are, however, some advantages, such as the Irish hare, a bigger and separate subspecies to its British cousin, much like the mountain hare is. There are in fact two sorts of hare in Ireland, as the common brown hare has been introduced and survives in some numbers in the north-west.

Ireland, too, is much less populated than its neighbours and its farming is less intensive. Large areas of bog, scrubland, wetland, wood and hill survive to nurture and protect many wild animals. The otter, for instance, now under severe threat almost everywhere, thrives in Ireland, though it is not often seen other than by anglers and countryfolk going about their quiet ways.

Travelling along the Shannon–Erne waterway is in many respects one of the best ways to see a good cross-section of Irish wild animals. Water always attracts animals, either to drink or live nearby. The countryside around the waterway is comparatively unspoiled, well-forested and has plenty of wetlands and shrublands. As a result, wild animal life is rich.

The most common animals are the familiar ones – foxes, badgers, hedgehogs. Badgers are very numerous and you don't have to be too skilled to notice them, but seeing them in the flesh is a different matter. The badger digs tremendous holes called setts in which to live, usually in woodland, scrub or even field ditches,and these are all too easily visible once you decide to look for them.

They are creatures of habit, taking the same trails night after night as they emerge to feed, so it is easy to track them. One of the best ways of seeing them is to drive slowly around the lanes at night, when one will often be seen ambling along the roadside.

This half-eaten fish could be evidence of otters by the waterway

Foxes are very plentiful – too plentiful, many farmers would allege. The fox is a clever and astute animal who has adapted to the ways of man rather than the other way round and the urban fox living in the very heart of cities and towns is a familiar sight in Ireland also. The best time to see a fox is early on a summer's morning.

Ireland strangely has no weasels, though country folk still call the stoat a weasel. Stoats are quite common and the best place to see them is by the roadside. They like stone walls and will often stop and stare at humans, showing little fear. The Irish stoat is a separate sub-species which is also found in the Isle of Man, and the further north one gets in Ireland, the smaller the stoat becomes. Since the dreadful rabbit disease myxomatosis was introduced to Ireland in the fifties, stoats, like rabbits, have declined in numbers.

The most prized experience with Irish wild animals, however, is sighting the otter. Although otters are widespread – much more than most people imagine – they are difficult to see. Most anglers walking or wading quietly by a river or lake will have seen them; the author once, while fishing, came across two large otters playing on a gravel bank beside a midland river and watched them for almost an hour before they went away.

They are most common on the west coast, where they are quite easily seen swimming and hunting in the sea, but are found beside any water which has enough fish and above all, eels (the otter's favourite food) to support them. Watch for their distinctive droppings, known as spraints; these are full of fishbones, which give them a sort of spiky look, and they also smell fishy – you'll find them on rocks and prominent places beside the water.

One very rare animal is found along the waterway, or at least in some parts of it, notably at Crom estate, where they were discovered a few years ago. This is the pine marten, Ireland's rarest mammal, which is shaped like a stoat and about the size of an ordinary cat. The pine marten is mostly limited to the west and north-west, though he is also found in other places around Ireland.

Like the mainland of Great Britain, Ireland has a problem with declining numbers of red squirrels. It used to be the only squirrel in the country, but since the grey squirrel was introduced in County Longford in 1911 it has spread rapidly and has more or less usurped and replaced its red cousin.

The grey is a more active breeder and a more aggressive colonizer than the red and has squeezed the latter out of much of its former habitat. It is still found throughout the country but in much reduced numbers, while another difficulty in seeing it is that it is shy and retiring, unlike the grey squirrel, which is much more easily seen. However, along the Shannon–Erne waterway there are still plenty of red squirrels; watch for them in coniferous woodland.

Another animal now accepted as a wild species is the American mink. Mink used to be farmed in quite large numbers for their skins. Being clever and adaptable animals, many have escaped and made a life for themselves in the wild. Indeed, most Irish mink are now wild.

The mink has an awesome reputation as a destroyer of fish, but in fact it is a poor, slow swimmer and would not have a chance of catching a healthy fish in its own watery element. Instead it eats whatever it gets – a real scavenger and quite often seen by the waterside. It is easy to tell an otter from a mink; the otter is very much larger and is more browny-coloured, while most mink are blackish. Otters, too, are much more wary of man; the mink will often show little or no fear of humans when encountered.

The goat, too, has converted itself back into a wild animal. The more remote areas of Ireland, particularly islands, often abound in wild goats and there are several islands on the waterway, including Inishfendra, where they now live.

The country's deer have tried hard to live up to the legendary and mythical Irish elk. There are three species: the red, fallow and sika deer. The sika hardly qualifies as a native deer, having been brought to Ireland in the nineteenth century, but it has settled in well and is found both in Fermanagh and Tyrone, its neighbouring county.

The red deer survives and is now prospering after having been almost wiped out. Once it was the most widespread of the country's deer but was hunted to near-extinction. Today it is found mostly in Kerry, Wicklow and Donegal, but it is beginning to extend into Fermanagh also.

The fallow is by far the most common of Irish deer. It was introduced to Ireland by the Normans, and most of the fallow deer in the country today are wild descendants of those first colonists. They are mostly found in forested land and the best place to see them close to the waterway is in Crom, where there is a herd of about 100 fallow deer in the estate woodlands.

By far the most common animal you are likely to see by the waterway, however, is one which is not widely regarded as an animal at all. Ireland has just seven species of bat (Britain has twice that), four of which at least are plentiful enough along the waterway – pipistrelles (the most abundant), brown long-eared, Daubenton's and Leisler's.

Two Great Houses

Rising straight from the green grass of Fermanagh, almost as though it had grown from it as organically as the trim trees which set off its perfect lines, Castle Coole is one of the finest houses in the island of Ireland. It is, by common consent, certainly the finest neo-classical house in the country, despite Dick Warner's reservations.

Like many an Irish house, Castle Coole reflects its history and its heritage in a diversity of ways. It is neither the first nor even the second house to establish itself on the site; in the seventeenth century a plantation castle was built there by an English official but was later destroyed in the rebellion of 1641.

After a wealthy Belfast merchant family, the Corrys, had bought the estate, a Dutch-style house was built in the early eighteenth century, only to burn down towards the end of the century. It was a case of third time lucky when the present Castle Coole was built for the Corrys at the end of the eighteenth century. By the time it was finished in 1797, the reigning Corry had been made Earl of Belmore.

The earl was nothing if not ambitious. He wanted a grand house for several reasons: first for himself and for his family, but also because, like many another before and since, he wanted desperately to keep up with the Jones, who in this case was his brother-in-law, the Earl of Enniskillen, owner of the superb Florence Court nearby. If brother-in-law had a fine house, then so must he.

Thus no expense was spared in making Castle Coole the equal of Florence Court. The architect Richard Johnston, a brother of the more famous Francis Johnston, and the man who designed the Gate Theatre in Dublin, was brought in to design the house, but no sooner had the foundations been laid than Johnston was fired, to be replaced by an even more illustrious architect, James Wyatt, then the darling of English society. However, although Wyatt did design the house from the basement up, and in fact visited Ireland once in 1785, he never actually saw his creation.

The house cost a fortune – £60,000, an astronomical sum in those days. It almost broke Lord Belmore, for when he died just a few years after it was finished he left debts of over £70,000. His son, however, carried on where father had left off, creating a lavishly furnished and decorated interior in the Regency Greco style. Nowhere was this more exemplified than in the room wherein lay – and lies – the elaborate State bed, made specially to receive the royal bulk of King George IV who, though expected to visit the castle, never came, a story which was be echoed in many another Irish house.

Castle Coole's beauties are many, both exterior and interior. Its strikingly handsome front is perfectly balanced by the flanking and graceful wings; its superb Portland stone-work is similar on all four sides, a rarity in Ireland, as more often than not the front only was concentrated upon. There are no fussy gardens, no shrubberies, no ornamentation to distract from the viewer's all-embracing gaze.

In the fifties the house and parkland were given to the National Trust, who have since spent millions on restoration and redecoration. On the lake near the house is a flock of greylag geese; they have the unique distinction of being the oldest non-migratory flock of greylags breeding in these islands. And they have another distinction: if they leave, 'tis said, so will the Corry family who created this wonderful house.

Its neighbour, Florence Court, has had a different and yet a similar history. Its setting is wilder, more Irish. Set off by the lowering backdrop of the Cuilcagh mountains, there is almost an untidy air to the land around the house, but this is what gives it a wonderful charm. The house was built before the flanking wings were added by a Sardinian architect, but the effect is magical, one of harmony and balance.

Florence Court was the home of the Earls of Enniskillen. The earlier house dates from about 1730, the wings are about forty years younger. Little is known about its architectural history, which is unusual in a house of its type, where normally great stress would have been laid on keeping meticulous records of house and estate.

Its chief delight is in its superb interior plasterwork, ornate yet delicate, flamboyant yet restrained. In the fifties, shortly after it was handed over to the National Trust by the Earl of Enniskillen, a disastrous fire all but gutted it. Most of the plasterwork was destroyed but that in the dining-room was saved by the quick action of a local builder, Bertie Pierce, who drilled holes in the plasterwork to allow the water which the firemen had poured on it to escape. The rest was recreated from photographs taken in 1915.

In the grounds of Florence Court, secreted in a clearing in the woods, stands a relic of the ages – the famous Florence Court yew tree. From this single tree, which can only be propagated by cuttings, the Irish yew spread right around the world.

Facing page: Castle Coole in County Fermanagh, one of the great classical houses of Ireland

A Way of Life

In India, high in the Himalayas, there is a secret and sacred place called Hardwar. Here people come to meditate. They remain alone, eating, sleeping and meditating. Nothing else.

They are practising yoga, as they were ordained to by Lord Krsna in the book which is at the very centre of Hare Krishna thinking, the *Bhagavadgita* (literally, the Song of God).

Krsna, or Krishna as it is pronounced and spelt in the west, simply means the height of pleasure. The Krsna guru, Swami Prabhupada, has described it thus: 'Each of us, every living being, seeks pleasure. But we do not know how to seek pleasure perfectly. With a materialistic concept of life, we are frustrated at every step in satisfying our pleasure because we have no information regarding the real·level on which to have real pleasure. To enjoy real pleasure, one must first understand that he is not the body, but consciousness …' Thus is outlined the very heart of Krsna.

The Bhagavadgita is to followers of Krsna as the Bible is to Christians, only, in this disbelieving and cynical age, more fervently and reverently followed and believed. It is one of the founts of Indian spiritual wisdom from a sub-continent renowned for its deeply

A Hare Krishna community

unique approach to the question of religions. In it, Lord Krsna, the Supreme Personality of Godhead, charts his followers' way along the road of philosophic and religious belief and meaning, much as Christ does in the Bible. It is, as is the Bible, a guidebook to the ultimate achievements in life – a true and complete happiness which is wholly spiritual and completely outside and beyond all material things.

Following the ways of Krsna is complex in the way that eastern religions are. At its centre is the practice of yoga. 'Yoga means control of the senses. If you indulge your senses unrestrictedly but make a show of yoga practice, you will never be successful.' To the followers of Krsna, yoga is the connecting link between the soul and the Supersoul, or the supreme and the minute living creatures, with Lord Krsna as the Supreme.

In the west, our familiar view of the Hare Krishna is as robed and shaven-headed monks, chanting and clanging cymbals as they rove along the streets of our towns and cities. In essence, while this physical description is accurate, it obscures the religious lives of those followers, a life which defines and illumines all they do. Unlike many Christians today, as Christianity's once strict standards are gnawed away by our modern and western conception of life, Hare Krishnas live their religion. It is, in effect, their lives.

Yoga is all-important in all of this as a form of meditation by which and through which the Hare Krishna reach at least some of their meditative goals. The idea is to get outside the body as it were, away from oneself to a contemplation of pure consciousness. Followers achieve this through yoga, by chanting the Hare Krishna mantra: Hare Krsna, Hare Krsna, Krsna, Krsna, Hare Hare, Hare Rama, Hare Rama, Rama Rama, Hare Hare.

'By chanting this transcendental vibration, we can cleanse away all misgivings within our hearts … the basic principles of all such misgivings is the false consciousness that I am the lord of all I survey.'

The reasoning is complex yet clear. 'By chanting, one can at once feel a transcendental ecstasy coming through from the spiritual stratum. In the material concept of life we are busy in the matter of sense gratification as if we were in the lower animal stage. A little elevated from this status of sense gratification, one is engaged in mental speculation for the purpose of getting out of the material clutches. A little elevated from this speculative status, when one is intelligent enough, one tries to find the supreme cause of all causes – within and without … and when one is factually on the plane of spiritual understanding, surpassing the stages of sense, mind and intelligence, he is then on the transcendental plane.'

Because its devotees often make themselves visible in a highly public way, Hare Krishna is a religion which is often misunderstood. It is a difficult and opaque one for westerners in particular to understand or even begin to appreciate; possibly, as many observant critics have noted, its true inner meaning is only fully appreciated by those who have been reared with an eastern religious ethos. But it is a religion of peace and tranquillity of soul and body – and what more fitting place for a community than an island in Northern Ireland?

Chapter 4

We're in a bit of trouble. Neither Declan nor I can keep *Oxlip* in steam long enough to make any real progress. We open the valve and set off across a stretch of water and the needle in the shiny brass gauge that tells us our steam pressure slides backwards till it reaches the 50 psi mark and we know we have to stop and either drift around or find a friendly beach, where we can run aground and wait a quarter of an hour while the needle inches back up again. And then another five or ten minutes of travelling and the whole process is repeated. So we admit defeat and send a message asking for David Laing, *Oxlip*'s owner, to come and care for the patient.

It has been raining a lot. In fact a hell of a lot. And when David arrives he says he reckons the problem is simply that our fuel has got too damp. But he says he'll run some checks, clean out her tubes and perform various other gynaecological operations, as well as getting some dry briquettes. This will take most of the day, so I decide to go sightseeing.

It's a strange place I end up in, up on the side of a limestone mountain overlooking the south shore of the lake. The limestone is built up like giant Lego, in blocks divided by joints and bedding planes. There are gorges, fissures in the surface of the hill, and water everywhere. Water spurts out of cliffs, disappears into holes in the ground, drips off the trees, lies in pools – and, if you put your ear to the rock, you can hear it rushing below you in underground arteries and veins.

When I climb into one of these gorges the air is very still and damp and neither cold nor warm. And this is a bit strange because it looks like a jungle and jungles should be hot. It's not just that there are trees and bushes. On the trees grows moss, and out of the moss grow epiphistic ferns, and over them grow strands of honeysuckle and lianas of briar. There is such a feeling of congestion. It's like plant rush-hour. Even the light is green.

I sit for a while trying to get used to the whole thing. At first I'm a little uneasy and look down to check that there isn't a bracket fungus growing from my shin or moss sprouting from my boot. Then I relax and begin to enjoy the place. And just as I'm really getting into it I'm reminded that enjoyment of this amazing landscape is not what I've come here for. This is the Marble Arch Caves and I'm supposed to be heading intrepidly into the bowels of the earth. OK.

There's a guide. Young but very competent-looking, festooned with gear like an old oak covered in polypody fern. A helmet with a cyclops light, of course, and rechargeable batteries hanging from a belt, and a first-aid kit, life-jacket, pouch for Mars bars, Swiss Army knife, survival manual, a lot of bits of rope and webbing which terminate in stainless steel karabiners and have no purpose I can work out. Yes, we're going to be all right.

Declan blows the steam whistle

Here's someone who knows what she's doing. She'll get me out alive.

I follow her orange anorak into a hole in the side of the hill. At first it doesn't seem real. Another theme park, cunningly crafted out of polystyrene and kevlar. That couldn't be stone. Stone doesn't flow like that. Look, there's a stone waterfall, a curtain of calcite flowing over a rib of real rock. But it is genuine and it is wonderful and I don't feel any claustrophobia, even when the ceiling dips and the walls close in. 'We were shut down last week,' she chats cheerfully over her shoulder. 'The caves flooded with all the rain. Where we're walking now was a river right up to the roof.' Maybe I feel a little bit of claustrophobia. But then the really good bit starts.

We worm our way round a corner in this underground intestine and the water is there and my heart gives a little jump. But it's all right, it's all part of the tour. This is a long, black, winding, subterranean lake … and it's got a boat on it. An aluminium skiff with an electric trolling motor clamped to one blunt end. We're going to travel by boat along an underground waterway.

In ancient Greece the dead were buried with two small coins called obols, one on each eyelid. This was because travelling to the next world involved a boat journey across an underground river called the Styx. The obols were to pay the fare to the ferryman, who was called Charon. By a rather shivering coincidence my ferryperson is called Sharon. And I haven't got two obols on me.

Never mind. Sit back and enjoy the strangest boat journey in Ireland. The scenery is certainly interesting. I try to decide if it's also beautiful. The water-worn rock and the spines and flows of calcite are very sculptural. The shapes are fascinating, sometimes pleasing. But there's nothing living – apart from the ferryperson, myself and a solitary bat winging through a beam of electric light. It is the total opposite of the green riot at the cave mouth. And, for me, scenery without life can never be really beautiful.

So I'm quite happy when we're dazzled by the light of a dull afternoon as we re-emerge into the world of the living.

On the drive back to Enniskillen I stop to admire a wet meadow beside the road. What first catches my eye are the flowers. Campions and red and yellow loosestrife, meadowsweet, flowering rush and the big seed-pods of flag iris. I even find what I think is one of the rarities of wet Fermanagh, a white umbellifer called cowbane … umbellifers are tricky plants, and I haven't got a flora with me, but I'm about 80 per cent sure of my identification.

After a while I start to look at the meadow differently. I change my eyes from what television calls a close-up to a wide-shot and try and take in the totality of what I'm looking at. The flowers that first caught my attention are very much in a minority, concentrated around the wetter margins. The meadow is really a sea of grass … or, if I move back to the close-up, of grasses. The sea has waves as puffs of breeze blow across it. And the grasses have seed-heads and there is a bewildering variety of them. The wet meadows of Fermanagh are one of the few places in Europe were grass is not cut in its nutritive adolescence but allowed to mature and flower, because the meadows themselves don't dry up enough to support mowing equipment until quite late into the summer. This is the reason why the corncrake found one of its last nesting havens in Fermanagh … at least, up until last year; in 1994 the corncrake was officially declared extinct in Northern Ireland.

I start to collect grasses and soon end up with nearly a dozen species which are completely different. Some have seed-heads like a fox's tail, some are like an ear of oats, others bristly cones of fibre, or flat daggers, or feathery Christmas trees. This one's Timothy grass, named after the man who introduced it to the ranchers of North America, and this one's quaking grass and I really haven't an idea what the rest are called. It doesn't really matter. You don't have to be able to put a name to the various species to appreciate their bewildering variety and to wonder what ecological imperative forces so much diversification in such a small acreage.

Rush hour in Fermanagh

Enniskillen: the town stands on the River Erne. Portora Boat Club is in the foreground, on the left.

Rich, natural meadows are one of the most endangered habitats in Ireland, and in the whole of Europe. They are now so rare that it's quite a shock to come across one and be confronted by the complexity of its natural history.

It's some time since I've walked around a town, and Enniskillen is far and away the largest place on the whole journey. So at first I find it a little disconcerting. Traffic drives on the left, which is the opposite way round to the waterway, and a couple of times I find myself looking the wrong way as I step off the kerb, like any bumpkin. But it's a very pretty town with two bridges and a waterside castle and a shopping street which is a control zone, which means that if you leave a car unattended the security forces may blow it up. At night the street is closed off by barriers, also for security reasons. I am fascinated by the barriers themselves. They are intricately cast pieces of iron, painted black and gold. Real works of art. I find it puzzling but admirable that the authorities should take something as utilitarian, even sinister, as a security barrier and make it beautiful.

I take my tanned and bearded face, with its odd accent, into a couple of shops to buy essential supplies – whiskey, tobacco, *The Irish Times*. People are friendly and the prices of most things are a good bit less than in the Republic. I feel like a foreign tourist … and that may be rather a profound feeling, considering what arguments there are about whether the island of Ireland contains two nations or one.

On the far side of town, planted haughtily on a high hill, is Portora Royal School, a Protestant boarding-school established to educate the sons of the middle classes. Scions of the big houses were sent to English public schools. Catholics and the working class knew they need not apply. But the offspring of clergymen, lawyers, doctors and strong farmers went to Portora … still do.

Samuel Beckett played on the school cricket team. There is a photograph of him in a cricket cap, striped blazer and flannels. I think the picture might have appealed to his love of the bizarre. And Oscar Wilde went to school here … but after the trial they removed his name from the list of alumni and didn't speak about him for the best part of 100 years.

I walk through beech trees, down flights of steep steps that lead from the school to its rowing club on the river. I am waiting for Declan to collect me here in *Oxlip*. It's a sunny early morning and birds are singing. Last night at midnight the IRA declared a cease-fire. I dump my gear and stretch out on the warm boards of the landing stage, lighting a pipe full of cheap Northern Irish tobacco. Life seems pretty good … until a burst of automatic weapons fire coming from about eighty yards away across the river. Then more. Random shots. A fire fight. Well within range.

I abandon my gear and rush for the steps. What irony. All these weeks in Northern Ireland and the first violence comes the morning after the cease-fire. The steps are very steep. And there's lots of them. My breath is giving out and I'm trying to keep the solid trunks of beeches between me and the firing, which is still going on. And as I get winded I get more scared. I know what I'm hearing. I've heard it before. God, it's steep.

I arrive at the top in something of a panic and try and communicate with the television crew, who are up there preparing the camera ... 'Take ...' pant, wheeze ... 'take cover ...' gasp ...'automatic weapons, take cover ...' pant, blow, whistle ... 'shooting, across the river ...' This pantomime goes on for nearly a minute, the television crew gazing at me curiously and wondering if they should call a doctor. Then a senior boy from the school, in a crisp grey uniform, strolls across and says: 'It's a police practice range. They start at nine every morning. They should be finished in about half an hour.' I walk slowly and foolishly back down the steps to my gear.

Below Portora the river is lined by large oak trees. Fine oaks have been a characteristic of the banks since I entered the Upper Lough at Crom. The oak is the Irish national tree – and probably the British too, come to think of it. Why? They are symbolic of massive strength, solid reliability, wise old age. Which is all rather specious because oaks almost never reach 300 years of age, are particularly susceptible to lightning strike and various forms of rot and disease, and produce rather indifferent timber in terms of density, durability or beauty. They were, however, the dominant species of the natural climax vegetation of acid soils in Ireland. On sweeter soils they gave way to ash, yew and elm; while pine, birch, rowan and aspen took over in the mountains.

This does give them a considerable significance, particularly if you learn to look at them properly. When I look at an oak tree, or a grove of oaks, I think of them not as individual organisms but as ecosystems. They live in symbiotic conjunction with a host of fungi, mosses and ferns. Several hundred insect species are directly and completely dependent on them – and that includes the purple hairstreak, Ireland's most exotic and elusive butterfly. Without oaks we would find it difficult to support our remaining jays and squirrels. And when we felled most of our oak forest we lost our wild boars and our woodpeckers.

I talked recently to Cormac Foley, a man with great wisdom about trees who is involved in the management of the largest remaining oak wood in Ireland, round Killarney in County Kerry. He'd spent some years puzzling about the problems he was having getting native oak trees to regenerate. And he came up with an intriguing answer. 'The problem, Dick,' he told me, 'is lack of pigs. At one time we had wild boars. When they became extinct, domestic pigs were pastured in the woods under rights of pannage. These pigs rooted and ploughed under the oak trees, as pigs will, and they created the right conditions for acorns to germinate in. Now they're gone and I can't get my oaks to reproduce.'

I find this interesting, it illustrates the complexities of nature, in the same way that Enniskillen, on the strategic isthmus between the two lakes, illustrates the complexities of culture. *DW*

Underneath the Arches

The rock formation of Ireland is a complex and intricate jigsaw. The first pieces went into position perhaps 200 million years ago, the final ones just tens of millions of years ago. And age and weather and other factors have continued their slow work of evolution and change since then.

Between 400 and 600 million years ago, in what is known as the lower Palaeozoic era, a huge ocean covered that part of the earth's surface where Ireland sits today. This ocean was called Iapetus after the Greek father of Atlas; in many ways, the ocean was the father of the present Atlantic Ocean.

Over time, this ocean built up huge deposits of sand and mud washed in from other, distant lands, gradually narrowing the Iapetus as the continental masses which bordered the ocean on either side advanced inexorably towards each other. Finally these great land masses collided, crushing each other in an unimaginably powerful impact. The marine sediments between them were pushed upwards into great folds and hills whose pleated rucks and dips ran north-west to south-east, high above the surrounding surfaces. This enormous upheaval was accompanied by granite magma which thrust up strong pillars from deep within the earth's crust in present-day Galway, East Leinster, Newry, Donegal and Mayo.

As the millennia unfolded, this raw landscape began slowly to change. Weather began its inexorable work of erosion. The sands and gravels were carried by rivers southwards and deposited as sandbanks on rivers and lakes, creating vast alluvial floodplains as they progressed. By the end of the Devonian period, the huge mountains which had been created some 65 million years earlier had been eroded to sea-level and now a new ocean began to form, burying the continental sediments and creating what we now know as red sandstone.

Later on, sediments and mud which were rich in lime content formed slowly over about 20 million years in the shallow lower carboniferous seas. Later these would harden into rock, creating the carboniferous limestone which forms so much of Ireland.

As the upper carboniferous period succeeded the lower, plants began to appear, to die and become compressed into coal. As the carboniferous eras faded, more continental collisions across Europe folded up the old carboniferous sediments and the old red sandstone which lay underneath them. New and rough mountains rose as a result, this time folding from east to west.

This is the basis of Ireland's rock formation. Most of the flattish midlands, a sort of bowl surrounded by low, worn hills for much of its borders, is underlain by carboniferous limestone. On the other hand, the great hills of Munster are primarily of old red sandstone; Dublin, Wicklow and Carlow are granite-based. In between are relicts of the past, too, in the lower Palaeozoic foundation of that large tract of land between Dundalk, Belfast and Longford. Throughout the rest of Ireland, other much smaller and less significant formations occur.

The limestone basis of much of Ireland gives to it a unique appearance and structure. Limestone is not the hardest of rocks and is quickly eroded by wind and rain and water. Over the years, those parts which have been exposed to any of these forming influences twist and hollow and open into fantastic shapes and sculptural forms. The vast tracts of limestone which lie open to the wind and rain, such as the Burren in County Clare, not only create their own unique flora and fauna but their own strange shapes and corrugated surfaces as well.

Nowhere is this more evident than underground, where the influences of erosion, though hidden from the surface, are every bit as strong as those which are more exposed. The strongest of these by far is water. Ireland is never short of water, its hidden underground lakes and wells fed liberally by the gentle rain which falls for much of the year. Stored in soft limestone, the waters expand through devious means, creating as they do so some extraordinary underground effects.

It is a country rich in caves of all shapes and sizes, made over the years by the unceasing workings of water. Some of these caves are very large indeed, others small and insignificant. But, almost without exception, they owe their existence to two factors – the presence in Ireland of so much carboniferous limestone and the water which shapes and sculpts it.

Of all the many cave systems which this combination has created, the Marble Arch Caves near Florence Court in Fermanagh are the most spectacular. This part of Fermanagh is rich in limestone and when the ample rain falls (and Fermanagh people will swear it never stops!) on the Cuilcagh Mountains high above the caves, it leaches down through the peat bog which covers much of the slopes.

As it drips down through this sponge, the reaction of water and bog creates a mild acid which when it reaches the limestone plateau below, has the power to erode the softer areas of limestone. Rainwater itself is a very weak and diluted form of carbonic acid, formed when it takes up carbon dioxide from the atmosphere and humic acid from organic soils. The Cuilcagh peat slopes have added their own acids to this to make quite a strong acidic solution which, percolating through the vertical joints and horizontal bedding cracks in limestone, dissolves and cracks the rock. Sooner or later these tiny percolations unite to form little rivulets and streams, eventually to unite into a sizeable stream or river. It is this size and strength which has the capability of forming large underground caves.

In the case of the Marble Arch Caves, rainwater has done its erosive and creative job in a spectacular and vast fashion. The caves are most dramatic. At their heart is a river system, where three streams, the Pollasumera, the Owenbrean and the Sruh-Coppa meet to create a river, the Claddagh. Around this has been created a most diverse and surreal landscape of flat pavements, rivers which vanish down holes and reappear, high cliffs, deep craters, vast chambers, strange scallopings on the walls caused by water action, pillars of incredibly complex shapes and appearance, wonderful coloured and sculpted stalagmites and stalactites. First explored by E.A. Martel in 1895, using a flimsy collapsible boat, the caves are at the centre of a vast and wriggling network which winds and dives its snake-like way under the surrounding countryside.

The caves are open to visitors and, depending on whether it has been raining or not, you can even travel by boat on some of the underground waters. But whether dry or wet, they are worth exploring, if only to appreciate the immense natural forces which have created these underground wonders.

Marble Arch Caves in County Fermanagh

Enniskillen on the Erne

Unlike many things Irish, there is little dispute as to how the town of Enniskillen got its name. Inis, the Gaelic name for an island, and Ceithleann, the genitive case of Ceithle – there you have it.

But just who was Ceithle? Was he, as the Annals of Clonmacnoise would have it, a king of the legendary Tuatha de Danan or was Ceithleann a woman who was the wife of Balor, the one-eyed leader of the Formorian giants of ancient Ireland? Whatever the answer – and the true one is unlikely ever to be found – Enniskillen is probably named after Enniskillen Castle, where a castle of the great local Gaelic clan, the Maguires, stood from at least the fifteenth century.

The Maguires played as large a part in Enniskillen's history as they did through the rest of the county, and their own Enniskillen Castle serves as a microcosm of the ups and downs of their relationships with the Elizabethan settlers who came to Enniskillen in the sixteenth century. In 1594 the castle was captured and garrisoned by the English, and the Maguires were ousted. But back they came and retook the castle a year later. The English seized it once more and then, as if exhausted by the struggle, actually gave it back to the Maguires. In 1602 the original town was destroyed by an English force led by an Irishman, one of the O'Donnells, and a few years later the Maguires were once more ousted from the castle, this time permanently. It was taken over by Captain William Cole, and thus began the history of modern Enniskillen.

Enniskillen is perfectly situated on an island in the River Erne – one of the most beautifully positioned of all Irish towns. Its strategic position had always singled it out as of high military importance – hence the tenacity with which the Maguires held it for so many years. But when the English took it over it was granted by King James I to Captain Cole, whose family were to become Earls of Enniskillen, and became one of the strongest bastions of Protestant settlers in the whole of Ulster and indeed in Ireland. It was a rallying point for the Protestants in the Rebellion of 1641 and in 1689 it rallied strongly and effectively to the Protestant and anti-Catholic cause of William of Orange, who himself was to become the victor of the Battle of the Boyne, one of the most central battles in Irish history. Two of the most famous regiments in the British Army, the Royal Inniskilling Dragoons and the Royal Inniskilling Fusiliers, originated in the town.

Enniskillen today is very different to the town of the Maguires. None of the original buildings of the old town survive, which is hardly surprising in view of the almost unceasing wars which the place has had to endure. And not only wars but other disasters as well: twice, in 1695 and 1705, the town was more or less destroyed by fire, the latter one leaving 114 families – almost everyone in the town – homeless.

It was not until industrialization came that Enniskillen began to grow. In the eighteenth century a thriving linen industry had grown up and on the back of this industry in particular the town began to prosper.

Linen is one of the most famous Irish products. At that time, it was very much what is today called a cottage industry. Small and large farmers alike grew flax, the basic crop used in linen-making, and the cloth was then woven by thousands of women working in their own homes. It was tedious work – spinning, boiling, winding – but there was little or no other employment for women and the work was eagerly accepted. There was also a

Enniskillen Castle

seemingly insatiable demand for linen, and Enniskillen became something of a centre for the industry. There were separate markets for flax, for yarn and for the many kinds of bleached and unbleached linen cloth.

Enniskillen also became for a short while a centre for a similar but much smaller industry – cotton. It was set up by the Earl of Enniskillen in 1785 and produced corduroy, velveteen and quilted products. At one time, ten houses in the heart of the town were used in this industry, but it eventually petered out.

Not only industry prospered. Enniskillen's strategic location made it an ideal melting-pot for the great raw industry at which Ireland has always excelled – farming. The countryside around the town is rich in grass and dairying became a large industry, with Enniskillen serving as a huge butter market from which salted butter was shipped as far as Liverpool and Bristol – and even to such far-flung parts of the world as the West Indies, a vast distance and an even bigger undertaking in those days. At one time, in the first third of the nineteenth century, over 12,000 large casks of butter alone were shipped out of the town.

The arrival of the railway line into Enniskillen in 1854 gave a further impetus to the development of the area's agriculture. There now began a huge trade in the export of poultry, eggs, live cattle and pigs, which were shipped to England and Scotland after being railed to Belfast, Dundalk and Derry. A directory of trades which were being pursued in the town in 1839 gives some idea of what was going on there and what sort of activities were helping to make Enniskillen so prosperous – blacksmiths, brassfounders, cartwrights, feather merchants, leather cutters, skinners, tallow chandlers, tinsmiths, tanners, wheel-wrights, cutlers.

One oddity was an eel fishery. Lough Erne is rich in eels – there are still eel fisheries there today – and in the 1830s an eel weir at Killyhevlin, a mile or so (less than 2km) from the town, was producing between 700 and 1,000 dozen eels a year, most of which were eaten locally but some at least of which were salted, stored in casks and sold in neighbouring counties.

Today, Enniskillen reflects its rich and varied history in a way that few Irish towns can equal. One sobering aspect which strikes the visitor is the control zone which cordons off the centre, but in many ways this too seems in some way to be in keeping with a town which has seen so much strife between different beliefs and ambitions. The physical evidence is more welcomely alive in the variety of buildings, many of them religious. Perhaps it is symbolic that two of the finest are the Protestant cathedral, a fine Gothic building, and the Catholic St Michael's – standard-bearers for two cultures which have retained their identity throughout Enniskillen's long and disturbed history and which, in today's hopeful climate, may well herald a more peaceful and settled era. Enniskillen deserves at least that much.

A School for Scandal

'My eldest boy is nearly eleven – very clever and very high-spirited,' wrote a woman to a close friend on 22 April 1863, 'and tho' he obeys me he will scarcely obey a governess. I feel it would be a risk to leave him. But we think of sending both boys to a boarding school soon …'

The woman was Lady Jane Francesca Wilde. The eldest boy was William Wilde. And the other boy was Lady Jane's youngest son, Oscar.

The Wildes were a very well-known family indeed. Lady Jane came from a Wexford Protestant family, the Elgees. She was to become, under the pen-name Speranza, one of the best known poets, essayists and polemicists of her day, imbued with strong opinions and fervid nationalist sentiments.

William Wilde senior, her even better-known husband, who was knighted in 1864, was, like his wife, a remarkable person in his own right. He was by common consent the greatest eye and ear doctor of his generation in Ireland, contributing definitive textbooks which were the foremost of their kind for many years. Today surgeons still use such terms as Wilde's incision, Wilde's cone of light and Wilde's cords. He was also a writer of note – his *Beauties of the Boyne and Blackwater* and also *Loch Corrib* are classics of their kind – and an archaeologist, cataloguing the huge collection of antiquities now in the National Museum in Dublin.

In between these achievements, Wilde had other, less favourable, attributes. Dublin was a-buzz with strange stories of his doings and misdoings. One story related how he once removed both eyes from a patient and put them on a plate, intending to replace them. But he forgot about them for a few hours, during which they were eaten by a cat …

Another story relates a well-known riddle which went about Dublin: why are Sir William Wilde's nails so black? To which the answer was: because he has scratched himself. He was the centre of much of Dublin society and knew all the great people of his day. The Wildes were noted for their huge and extravagant parties and soirées, to which fashionable Dublin thronged and gossiped.

There was plenty to gossip about. Both William and Lady Jane had their dark side. Besides being a brilliant, if eccentric, doctor, and for all his many cultural and academic attributes, Wilde was also a libertine of the first order – before he was twenty-three he had fathered at least three illegitimate children, and in later years saw little reason to change his behaviour. Lady Wilde was no angel either, once remarking, when she was in her sixties, to a much younger man: 'When you are as old as I, young man, you will know there is only one thing in the world worth living for, and that is sin.'

Small wonder that, with these two highly individual and even eccentric parents, Oscar

Wilde would, it was felt, be better off in a boarding-school. And so, along with older brother Willie, he was sent off to Portora in Enniskillen.

In 1608, a year or so after the last of the great native Irish chieftains had departed (the infamous Flight of the Earls), leaving the way now clear for full English control of the island of Ireland, the Privy Council in London gave detailed orders about how the plantation of all confiscated lands in the province of Ulster was to be carried out.

One of the many conditions laid down by the Council concerned education: 'There shall be one free school, at least, appointed in every county, for the education of youth in learning and religion.' That school in County Fermanagh was the Free School, based firstly in Lisnaskea, and later moving to Enniskillen, where at first it was known as the Royal School before changing to its present name, Portora Royal School.

Portora has been on the same site since 1777, overlooking Enniskillen from a high position to the north-west. With its motto, O*mnes honorate* (honour all men), it is one of the great schools of Ireland. As the school says of itself, it 'seeks to impress on every pupil the everlasting solidity of this ancient moot … Portora is also proud of its fine tradition as an Irish public school … while in no way compromising its religious and political origins, Portora is conscious that its pupils should be aware of the validity of the differing traditions within Irish society …'

For the Wildes, like many another set of parents from many parts of Ireland, Portora's wealth of tradition, firmly rooted in the concept of Protestant ascendancy but with a good dose of liberalism thrown in to soften it, was an ideal climate in which to educate their children. Oscar in particular excelled. He was an astonishingly fast reader, able to read and absorb a three-volume novel in half an hour. He was also a good, if lackadaisical, student who rarely had to work very hard to gain prizes, which soon began to come his way without real effort.

Above all, he shone at the classics. In his last two years in Portora he astonished both students and teachers alike by willingly making oral translations of Thucydides, Plato and Virgil – hardly the delight of most school students.

There are widely differing accounts of Oscar's years at Portora but many agree on one aspect – his penchant for elaborate and flamboyant dressing, going about in scarlet and lilac shirts and even, alone among the boys, wearing a silk hat on weekdays. But his dandyism never got in the way of his scholastic achievements, of which there were many. In 1870 and 1871, for instance, he won the Carpenter Prize for Greek Testament and then a scholarship to Trinity College, Dublin.

There were, however, to be black spots in Wilde's association with his old school. Having won his Trinity scholarship, his name was placed in gilded letters on the famous notice board in the school on which all such honours are recorded. In 1895, when the full scandal of Wilde and his homosexual affairs was revealed at the infamous London trial instigated

Oscar Wilde, from a Spy cartoon of the 1880s

by the Marquess of Queensberry, the father of Lord Alfred Douglas, one of Wilde's lovers, the school erased the gilded name. Even the initials OW which Oscar had carved by the windows of one of the classrooms were scraped away by the headmaster himself.

Today, the name of Oscar Wilde has been regilded and replaced on the school board and Portora, as it should be, is intensely and rightly proud of one of its more famous alumni.

Another and equally illustrious boarder at Portora was Samuel Beckett, who, like Wilde, came from Dublin. Both were extraordinarily gifted writers but there the resemblance ends. Unlike Wilde, who abhorred all sports and refused to play any at all during his years at Portora, Beckett was an avid and excellent sportsman, playing as a star fast bowler on the Portora school cricket eleven, serving very ably as a member of the back line in the rugby side, becoming the school's light heavyweight boxing champion and a swimming champion as well. He was a senior prefect, a librarian and an excellent debater.

Beckett, however, did not fit in well otherwise at Portora. He was known to some teachers as 'Inky Sam' because his work was so untidy. His academic record is indifferent, unlike Wilde's brilliant career. He carried on an endless feud with one of his teachers, Mr Tetley, who taught – or tried to teach – the reluctant Beckett both maths and science. Beckett, like Wilde, had a clever, cutting and frequently malicious tongue and pen, and Mr Tetley appears to have come out signally the worst of their many encounters.

Beckett was later recalled by some of his school contemporaries as being a moody and even withdrawn boy who made few friends at school. Increasingly Beckett seemed to reject the very values and the society which the school stood for. For can there be any greater contrast between the schoolboy world of Portora, filled with hope and ambition, and Beckett's bleak and futureless *Waiting for Godot*?

However, Beckett did carry one aspect of his school career right through the many decades of his own long life. When Fergus Linehan of the *Irish Times* was allowed to see the great man in Paris in the eighties – a privilege accorded to very few people indeed – he saw to his surprise that the picture which dominated Beckett's Parisian apartment was not a Picasso or a Klee, or indeed anything of much note.

It was, instead, a picture of the then outside half on the Irish rugby team, Ollie Campbell. Beckett revered him, revered the Irish rugby team, revered rugby itself; and Linehan recalls that they spoke more of rugby than of anything else – it was the one subject about which the great man showed any animation.

For that at least, Portora could be said to be responsible. A pupil will take from any school what he or she will, and Wilde and Beckett, in their own widely differing ways, are proof of that old and wise axiom of education and life.

The Oak and the Ash

What shall we do for timber?
The last of the wood is down,
There's no holly nor hazel nor ash here
But pastures of rock and stone,
The crown of the forest is withered,
And the last of its game is gone.

(Irish writer Frank O'Connor, translated from the Gaelic)

In the late sixteenth century, the English government in Ireland proposed a scheme to employ over 4,000 soldiers for an unusual task; they were to protect the thousands of workers already there who were busy chopping down the woods in Munster. There are no figures to show just how many men were wielding axes but a protective force of 4,000 soldiers alone gives us some idea of just how vast an undertaking this was.

It was not the first of its kind. At the end of the fourteenth century King Richard of England had tried and failed to mobilize about 2,500 native Irish to cut down their own trees; but 'it was impossible to be affected while the leaves lay upon the trees, but after that time, when the trees were bare, then to burn the woods would be the next best means to do service upon him …'

The Erne basin still has many fine stands of oak trees

That one sentence reveals much. It shows that the steady process of reducing the woods which once had covered most of Ireland was already well under way at least six centuries ago (though in fact the methods described above were not, let it be said at once, responsible for that), and also that most of the woodland was deciduous trees—oaks, elms, alders, birch.

It was a slow process at first but then quickened frighteningly fast. In 1600, about one-eighth of the whole surface of the island of Ireland was forested. Two hundred years later, that proportion was just one-fiftieth. Exploitation of the woods, particularly of the ever-prevalent oak for a huge variety of purposes, meant the end for the vast hardwood forests of Ireland; and they have never recovered – in fact, Ireland has the lowest density of trees in Europe today.

Even those sober statistics do not tell the full story. For instance, to say that one-eighth of the country was under woodland in 1600 is in itself slightly misleading. Much of Ireland, mostly its high mountains and the rough limestone plains in Clare, as well as its extensive bogs, can be left out of the calculation; thus the figure of one-eighth of all potentially usable agricultural land as being forested is an under-estimation. The true figure is probably closer to one-fifth.

Ireland has an ideal climate for growing trees – relatively mild, wet and without extremes of hot and cold. Its woods date from the time when the climate began to get milder after the last ice age. The so-called native species then began to flourish – hazel, elm, oak, ash, yew, pine, birch, willow, rowan or mountain ash, holly, alder, whitebeam. Oddly enough, the great trees which later became such a feature of the controlled parkland afforestation of the big country estates in the eighteenth and nineteenth century, such as beech, chestnut and lime, and also the poplar, were not introduced to Ireland until the Cromwellian plantation in the mid-seventeenth century, although the black poplar is now thought to be native.

Of all the trees associated with Ireland, none is more fascinating than the Irish yew, known taxonomically as *Taxus baccata fastigiata*. The Shannon–Erne waterway is fortunate in having at least one remarkable specimen, the one in the woods at Florence Court near Enniskillen, which is said to have spawned all Irish yews from the eighteenth century onwards. But in the Crom estate on the shores of Upper Lough Erne is something even more remarkable, in the shape of two ancient yews believed to be in or around 1,000 years old, proving that the yew, in one form at least, has been in Ireland for a very long time indeed. These two are undoubtedly the oldest yews in Ireland.

Yew plays a particularly well-defined role in Ireland. In medieval times in particular it was closely associated with sacred sites, churches and graveyards. At least one large town, Newry in County Down, is named after the Gaelic version of the yew, *iubhar*, the name said to originate from the claim that it was St Patrick who actually planted the yew tree there.

The Irish yew has been propagated throughout the world from the original specimen in Florence Court in Fermanagh

That original tree was burned down in 1162 and another well-known and sacred yew, at the monastic site of Clonmacnoise on the River Shannon in the midlands, was destroyed by lightning in the twelfth century.

The prevalence of the yew in those times is remarkable. Giraldus Cambrensis, the Welsh monk of royal links who travelled through Ireland in the twelfth century, wrote: 'Yews, with their bitter sap, are more frequently to be found in this country than in any other place I have visited; but you will see them principally in old cemeteries and sacred places where they were planted in ancient time by the hands of holy men, to give them what ornament and beauty they could.'

Mark the phrase – 'the ancient time' – and recall that Geraldus was writing in the twelfth century!

That the oak was by far the commonest tree in old Ireland is indisputable. The Gaelic name for an oak is *dair*, and today there are well over 1,500 townlands in the country with the word derry, an anglicized derivation of *dair*, somewhere in them, either as prefix or suffix – a singular tribute to the widespread presence of the oak.

It is particularly prevalent in the area of the Shannon–Erne waterway, with about a third of all the 'derries' occurring in Fermanagh, Leitrim, Cavan, Longford, Roscommon, Monaghan and Armagh. Lough Erne at one time was certainly one of the most densely wooded parts of Ireland, and most of those woods were oak.

Although the denudation of the woods of Ireland really began in earnest with the Cromwellian settlers, it would only be fair to say that the native Irish themselves had also been hard at it for some centuries as well. Timber was used in making houses and tools and was also used for firewood. Farming was steadily expanding and woodland would have been cleared to make room for crops of corn as well as for grazing. The grazing of herds of cattle, sheep and in particular goats – a death knell to all trees – caused further damage. But it was only in the seventeenth and eighteenth centuries that wholesale clearance began to alter the entire physical face of the land.

There were many reasons for this. Quite apart from the commercial value of the oak in particular, forests posed a big threat to the security of the English settlers and military. Natives could and did hide in the woods, from which they could launch attacks on their oppressors and afterwards melt back into them, there to be safe and secure from any pursuit.

One Elizabethan settler wrote in 1601:

'The woods and bogs are a great hinderance *(sic)* to us and help to the rebels – much good could be done by Irish churls felling, dressing, and burning the trees in heaps. This could be done whilst leaving sufficient timber for the use of the country, if a tree is left standing every twenty yards. Many people think it would have been well if Ireland had been turned into a seapool than have so charged Her Majesty …'

Another, and more sombre, aspect was that of the fate of the native woodkerne, or a man who lived in the woods. Actual manhunts were organised by the colonists, particularly in Ulster and even more particularly around Lough Erne. One writer of the time (1610) said of the manhunt, 'no doubt it will be a pleasant hunt and much prey will fall to the followers,' while Sir William Stewart of Newtownstewart in Co. Tyrone, just a few miles from Lough Erne, wrote as late as 1683:

'The gentlemen of the country have been so hearty in that chase that of thirteen in the county where I live, in November the last was killed two days before I left home.'

The same fate befell another resident of the woods. Wolves were prevalent in Irish woods and professional wolf-hunters were employed to keep their numbers down. It took them a long time to clear Ireland of wolves; in England,they were extinct well before 1500, but the last Irish wolf was killed in 1770.

Today, the woods of Lough Erne appear still to be quite extensive – as indeed they are in Irish terms. But it is not so long ago that things were very different. In 1700, for instance, just three centuries ago, the western shore of the lake north of Enniskillen was so wild and dangerous that it was 'scarce inhabited by any human creature but the O's and Mac's who pillaged all who came their way'. The natives could hide with ease in the huge forests of oak and ash, some at least of which remain.

The demise of the Irish woods came with the spread of industrialised practices. It was in the sixteenth century that wood began to appear on the lists of items exported from Ireland, which hitherto had consisted mostly of fish, salted hides, wool, linen and other items. Using wood as a fuel for the many ironworks which began to sprinkle the country became common practice but there were other uses – housebuilding, particularly in the seventeenth century before the more modern usage of brick and stone; shipbuilding; glassmaking; coopering and several others.

Coopering provides an interesting example of how wood was used. Barrels and casks are made entirely of wood, other than the iron hoops which hold them together. Ireland was a major producer of the staves, or planks, used in cooperage, and these were a huge export trade. Oak makes a superb stave and thus was used in barrels which held meat, butter, tallow, fish and so on.

Shipbuilding was never at any time a large industry in Ireland, though some wood was exported to England and even to Spain to build ships there. There is evidence to show, however, that it was more common sometimes to import wood into Ireland to build ships rather than the other way round. However, the boats used in Ireland on the rivers and lakes were all home-grown as it were.

Lough Erne, like many other areas, had its own indigenous designs, one of which was a sort of dugout canoe fashioned from an entire tree trunk. A sixteenth-century account refers to these as 'made from one tree … being such as would carry ten men the piece'. On the Shannon itself, there were boats called cots which could carry sixty men, and a cot excavated in Galway was some fifty feet long.

The other uses to which oak in particular was put, such as housebuilding, also took their toll. The Elizabethan colonization in the sixteenth century meant that many new Irish towns and villages were built, mostly in the then-current English fashion of half-timbering, with the interstices between the wooden timbers filled with bricks and mortar. Ulster planters, for instance, were allowed 200 good oaks to make whatever buildings they choose to erect as an added incentive to take on land and a living in Ireland.

One town built largely of oak around this time was Derry: 150,000 oak trees priced at ten shillings (50p) each and 100,000 elms (probably imported, as the elm had by then largely died out in Ireland) at six shillings (30p) each were earmarked to build 200 houses at first, with provision for another 300 in later years (many of these, in fact, were never built).

Ironworks also ate deeply into Ireland's woods. Ireland is rich in iron ore and nowhere more so than along the Shannon–Erne waterway, where one of the largest hills in the area is Slieve Anierin, the Iron Mountain. At one time at the height of Irish iron-making in the seventeenth and eighteenth centuries, there were over 150 ironworks in the country.

Young oak is the best wood for smelting iron ore and so the woods once more took an intense hammering. It takes twenty-five years of coppicing one acre of oak to provide enough fuel to make one ton of iron, so it can be seen that immense amounts of oak forest were needed to keep the furnaces going. The famous iron works near Drumshanbo in Leitrim, close to the waterway, elicited a report in 1770 which said that the works was ringed with heaps of charcoal as big as three Dublin houses. Sir Charles Coote, who kept a string of ironworks in Cavan, Leitrim and Roscommon, had 2,500 ironworkers alone.

Today, the picture of Irish woodlands is at first sight something of a bleak one. For many years, since the foundation of the new State earlier this century, the policy of growing trees, in itself an estimable one, was concentrated on conifers alone. The environmental disadvantages of vast areas of conifers now weigh heavily on afforestation policy, which is more and more geared to planting hardwoods. Enlightened policies and generous grants, particularly through the European Union, have meant that there is a more hopeful future for the Irish broadleaved hardwoods. But the climb will be a long and slow one and never again will we see, as the Irish did many centuries ago, areas of woodland so dense that a squirrel could cover fifty or a hundred miles by leaping from tree-top to tree-top and never touch the ground.

The sycamore, one of the many species seen along the waterway

Chapter 5

I'm not squeamish about animals. I'm not afraid of spiders or rats, I quite like snakes. But I'm cautious about eels.

They're a fascinating fish and, as an angler, I've had quite a few close encounters with them. But they bite you – not usually very hard, but it does transgress the etiquette of relations between the angler and his quarry. Also they wrap their strong bodies around your wrist and forearm and cover you with amazing quantities of slime. And once, fishing for sea trout with a worm in the dark, I made the mistake of trying to land an eel with a large-mesh landing net. It wove and knotted itself through the netting in a Chinese puzzle that took most of the night to untangle.

Jim Stephenson is the lock-keeper below Enniskillen. His lock is the gateway to Lower Lough Erne … and his job is one of the most enviable I've come across. A lovely house in a lovely setting with its own little harbour with a resident kingfisher … and the best bit is that the water levels between Upper and Lower Lough Erne vary so little nowadays that the lock hasn't been used for several years. So Jim has time on his hands.

He's a big, strong, competent sort of a man. A diver who goes down to repair moorings damaged in winter storms. A man with considerable skill in the art of living. He's also a fisherman. So is his son Arran, who tells me that he's paid for his mountain bike by selling perch and eels. And Jim's competence extends to the design and construction of a stainless steel fish-smoker, fuelled by smouldering alder logs. I eat his immaculately prepared eel, still warm from the smoker. It is probably the most delicious thing I've ever eaten in my life.

Then we push *Oxlip* away from the harbour wall, coil ropes, unfasten fenders and open the steam valve. We are heading for Lower Lough Erne and doing so slightly nervously.

Oxlip is a river launch. She tolerates canals well, and even enjoyed slipping from the lee of one island to the next on the Upper Lough. But Lower Lough Erne is daunting on the chart – an open expanse of water with little shelter. Locally it's called 'The Broad Lough'.

She's an open wooden boat, just over twenty feet long, and, because of the engine, boiler and water tank, weighs over a ton unladen. There is no built-in buoyancy. She doesn't rise to a wave, she ploughs through it. And, if enough water came on board, she would sink under us within minutes. The waves in the Broad Lough can, we are told, reach 5 feet (1.5m) in height.

As we steam on from the lock the nervousness seems a little silly. There is plenty of shelter, narrow channels, lots of islands. It's all rather like what we've already been through. We pass Devenish Island. A round tower and churches, relics of the medieval and

The Broad Lough: Lower Lough Erne and Oxlip under full steam

pre-medieval monastic tradition. Usually places like this fascinate me. They fuel my imagination with images of tonsures, robes and Latin chants. But Devenish is a disappointment. The Northern Ireland Department of the Environment has groomed and manicured the site for tourists until it almost seems like a monastic theme-park rather than the real thing. The old stones look like polystyrene blocks. There is no sign of wild nature mounting a counter-attack on the works of humans. Nothing to inspire.

Anyway, what's on view today in Devenish belongs to a period when the Irish Church had become just a rather provincial out-station of Rome. A few centuries previously we had been the hub of Christian intellect.

So we point *Oxlip* on down the lake and, slowly, the islands begin to thin out and I start to believe that things will broaden.

Two islands covered in trees, looking like clumps of moss in the distant water, and between them is revealed a grove of masts, a parking-lot of hulls. The Lough Erne Yacht Club – stiff with history. This is also one of the few places in Ireland where you can be fairly certain of seeing Fairies … not little people but smallish Edwardian sailing yachts with fin keels. We see some as we turn towards the club. Their gunter-lug rig carries a huge mainsail on an impossibly long boom. This pushes them over to a big angle of heel in the stiff breeze, the heavy keel the only thing preventing a capsize. They're travelling very fast, about a half-dozen in a race. I watch them for a while and figure out that there's some sneaky tactical sailing going on. The big, low mainsail is ideally suited to that old dinghy racer's trick of stealing an opponent's wind. There's quite a bit of that happening.

The Fairy class is indigenous to Lough Erne and is still largely unchanged

The boats are not only fast, they're very beautiful and obviously quite fun to sail. It occurs to me that the construction of one-design sailing boats for enjoyable racing hasn't really progressed that much in nearly a century. There's also a fleet of Mirrors … a design from the 1950s. And some J24s – fin keelers which are direct descendants of the Fairies, from the late 'seventies or early 'eighties, I think. I'd rather sail a Fairy.

Maybe this is because *Oxlip* is a bit of an anachronism too. I give the Fairies a toot on the steam whistle as we nudge our way through the race (steam giving way to sail) and approach the yacht club, looking for relics of more recent archaeology than that of Devenish Island.

The red-brick hangars and the concrete slipways of the Second World War flying-boat base are very evocative. There are details that reveal British craftsmanship of a period when Scunthorpe, Sheffield, Birmingham and Wolverhampton, not to mention Belfast, knew that they were world leaders, that they had standards which would not be dropped, even under the pressures of wartime.

And there are strong echoes across half a century of Britons, Canadians and Yanks. Young aviators flying their crates out over the Atlantic, looking for battle.

There was a war on here, a unique war. What made it unique was that it was the only one of the many wars fought in Fermanagh which wasn't directly concerned with who should own the green landscape immediately around the lake. This wasn't about clan and clan, Gael and planter, Catholic and Protestant. Suddenly war had grown into a multi-national.

And after the yacht club the Broad Lough does broaden. The horizon recedes and water sweeps in to fill the foreground … and the background … and everywhere. And I watch waves like I used to do when I was younger, skippering open boats on the Atlantic, judging how to climb a swell, when to turn, when to get frightened. As the landscape gets larger we get smaller, these are the simple laws of perspective. I am a little small, a little nervous, a little tired.

But White Island is achieved without incident and in enough time to pitch a tent and take a first look at the strange stone faces in the ruined church. The faces do not belong to the church. They have been discovered at various spots around the lake, mostly revealed on the shoreline when the water level has been dropped in the past by drainage or hydro-electric schemes. They have been placed in the church by the custodians of monuments, for safety and display. Cemented to a back wall of the ruin like traitors facing a firing squad.

Not a lot seems to be known about them. Originally they were described as pagan. Then someone pointed out the rather obvious fact that one was a portrait of a bishop. Now they are described as Christian. The distinction is probably not that important. What comes across is a feeling of primitive strength and a message across time from a culture very different to our own. I like these faces frozen in stone and spend a long time staring at them. They stare back.

I dream quite a lot in my sleeping-bag. I suppose it's only to be expected on an island with a ruined church where the only people are made of stone. And travel on down the lake the next morning towards Boa Island, and the strangest stone faces of them all.

Camp on White Island

On Boa Island is a graveyard called Caldragh which is very old. It was originally right on the shore, but then the lake level was dropped and now you have to scramble through 50 yards (metres) of holly trees and tall ashes, over boulders of limestone growing moss and ferns, in a green shade. When you get to the graveyard you know it's old because there are the remains of an oval stockade of quick thorns round it. Ancient thorns, black and white, providing the old Irish equivalent of a Masai *boma* to keep the cattle away from the dead. Some time later in history someone added a wrought-iron fence, painted black, and the thorn boundary was allowed to develop gaps.

This was the graveyard where all the island people from all over the Broad Lough ended their days. The hearses were boats and the grave-diggers had a hard time with the old shingle shore. It's maybe 1,000 years old and still in use.

But within Caldragh graveyard is something far older and more mysterious, placed there because graveyards are safe places to contain things which may have disturbing supernatural powers.

The Janus figures are smaller than I expected from the photographs I'd seen. One a bit over 2 feet (60cm) tall, the other maybe 3 feet (90cm) but they are not a disappointment. To call them Janus figures is, of course, wrong. Janus was a classical god, who gave us the month of January, with two faces – one looking backward to the old year, one forward to the new. The figures in the graveyard are not Roman or Greek and so are not representations of Janus … but they do have two faces. The faces of men, bearded like myself, with big heads, their arms crossed over their puny bodies. They face east/west, to the rising and the setting sun. But this is probably not very significant because they stand on concrete plinths and are obviously not in their original location.

A Boa Island figure: their origin and purpose are unknown

A man strolls down, the owner of the land, and tells me that the figures are 3,500 years old and that the stone they are made from does not occur naturally nearer than northern France.

He leaves and I wonder. I peer at the texture of the stone and wish I was a good enough geologist to know whether it had come from France. Each of the figures has a dip, a cup, at the top in which rainwater has collected. The man told me that it was for child sacrifices and hinted of recent strange rituals, with naked women lying on the stone slab in front of the idols. I dip my fingers in the rainwater and let it dribble through as I wonder.

The truth of the matter is that nobody knows anything at all about these figures. It is accepted that they are very old and rather powerful. Beyond that my imagination is free to speculate.... so here's what I got from my first encounter with them …

The Irish language is Celtic, and Irish people like to think of themselves as a Celtic race. The Celts were a barbarian and illiterate people who were really only interested in cattle and fighting. But before the Celts a mysterious and highly civilized race of neolithic tillage farmers inhabited this island for several thousand years. They were wealthy and highly organized, intellectuals who studied astronomy and had forms of writing and mathematical notation and were artists and architects in stone. These are the people who built Newgrange in County Meath, which, after more than 5,000 years, remains one of humanity's greatest monuments.

These people disappeared, leaving very little behind them. They were driven out by the superior war-skills of the invading Celts and nobody knows where they went … though the late Thor Heyerdahl had an intriguing theory that they crossed the Atlantic and founded the Mayan civilization in South America before being driven out again and carving great stone faces on Easter Island, *en route* to Polynesia. One of the few things we know about the Mayans is that they had pale skins and red beards.

I believe that the wonderful stone heads of Boa Island are one of the very few artefacts left behind by this Irish neolithic culture. And I find it interesting, if not conclusive, that the stone heads of Easter Island have cups on the top of the skull, just like the one the water from my fingers is dribbling back into.

Oxlip turns her stern to the conundrum of Caldragh cemetery and we head down the shore. Lower Lough Erne is in County Fermanagh, in Northern Ireland. But it is a little-known fact that a few yards of its shoreline around here actually lie in County Donegal, in the Republic. I nose the bow in gently, looking for rocks, trying to make a landfall in Donegal. Since the partition of the island in 1922 the spot, called 'The Waterfoot' because two rivers enter the lake here, has been busy with smugglers. But the rocky landing spot and the old drove road leading back from it are far older than 1922. For nearly 1,500 years pilgrims from all over the Christian world have been landing here after long and dangerous journeys and setting out up the road on the final few miles to Saint Patrick's Purgatory. I am going to do the same.

On the way I walk through the village of Pettigo, a disturbing experience. Pettigo is, I think, the only village in Ireland which is divided into two roughly equal parts by the border. There is a physical barrier of concrete and wire mesh, a wall, between the part of the village where the letter-boxes are green and the part where they are red. It's a quiet enough place as I walk through – neglected, even abandoned. When they took down the Berlin Wall they forgot about Pettigo.

Climbing from the village towards the mountains I come across something else which seems powerfully symbolic to me … another graveyard. It looks ordinary enough, up on the side of a hill. Again a little neglected, some recent burials and some very old ones. But if you stop to read the inscriptions on the stone you realize it's something quite unusual in Ireland. A graveyard where Catholics and Protestants are buried together.

In Pettigo they are divided in life. In this desolate cemetery they are united in death.

Saint Patrick's Purgatory is on an island in a mountain lake in Donegal called Lough Derg. There is, or was, a cave on the island and Saint Patrick took time off from converting the barbarian Celts to Christianity to meditate and pray in the cave. While there he had a vision of purgatory which seems to have motivated him strongly to go back to work … and was also the main influence on Dante when he wrote the Inferno.

It wasn't at all what I expected. The cave has gone. The island is completely built over, a mound of churches, dormitories, refectories and public toilets which spills over on piles and landfill into the surrounding lake. Pilgrimage to this place has not only got a long history, it has an active present. Thirty-two thousand pilgrams arrived in the 1994 season.

I come from a Protestant background. It's a background that finds it slightly odd to take off your shoes, fast for a day and a night and walk in circles over sharp stones, murmuring mantras and praying to statues. I mention this to Father Mohan, Prior of Lough Derg and parish priest of Pettigo, a man I take an instant liking to. He doesn't find it at all strange. He gets quite a few Protestants. The Reformation is something of a minor event on the timescale of this island. So I take off my shoes.

The effect is slowly cumulative and rather similar to dancing on Inis Rath with the Hare Krishnas. Discomfort becomes pain, repetition becomes numbing, concentration becomes focused into a smaller and smaller area … and then something happens which you could certainly describe as spiritual – and also as hallucinogenic. You alter your mind-state without recourse to drugs … and in a way which never seems threatening and is often strangely comforting.

There is no magic on Lough Derg. You could do the same thing in your own back garden. The magic is in your head, you import it with you along the pilgrim's way. But it's certainly a very effective setting for releasing inner magic.

Back in the sixties the advice given to people about to start a pilgrimage with LSD was 'set and setting, man'. The set was your mind-set, your state of mind. You needed to be reasonably calm and well-adjusted. The setting was the immediate environment in which you were going to have the experience and which, once the drug took effect, could either become threatening or beautiful.

Lough Derg is a good setting. *DW*

Island of Saints

In the National Museum in Dublin, there is a magnificent eleventh-century book shrine called the Soiscel Molaise. It's one of many similar fine antiquities housed in this treasurehouse of ancient Irish culture. But mark the name – Molaise.

Molaise was, and is, one of Ireland's best-known saints. Known popularly as one of the twelve Apostles of Ireland, a real distinction in an island once known as the Isle of Saints and Scholars, Molaise flourished in the sixth century. Based in Fermanagh, he was what's now known as a mediator, helping to sort out internecine tribal rows between truculent Ulster chieftains. And besides being a saint and a mediator, Molaise found time to run a monastery for about 1,500 students on Devenish Island in Lough Erne.

Though very different today to what it was in Molaise's heyday, Devenish still gives noble glimpses of its former religious and monastic grandeur. The fabled round tower, 80 feet (24m) high and with a panoramic view of the surrounding countryside (and a useful spot from which to spy an approaching enemy, of which there were many), is perhaps an over-exposed symbol of Devenish but it still serves as a potent reminder of bygone days. It was built in the twelfth century, probably to replace an earlier one nearby which may have been destroyed by plundering Vikings in the ninth century.

Devenish, though, is by no means all about the round tower. There are other fine remains, stony reminders of past glories. The ruined lower church, Teampall Mór, is full of history – a graveyard of the great local clan, the Maguires, and once a former Culdee monastery housing a strict anchorite order who also gave their name to nearby Killadeas. Then there is St Molaise's House, a much-ruined tiny church, and the ruins of St Mary's, an Augustinian priory dating from the middle of the fifteenth century.

Together, these stony remnants of a lost age and much-altered culture come across to the many thousands of visitors who arrive by boat each year. Though the days when 1,500 religious students thronged the island to over-capacity, and St Molaise ruled with wisdom and common sense, are long gone, there still lingers about Devenish and its ruins a tangible aura of its dimmed past.

The Fairies of Lough Erne

About a century and a half ago, a local newspaper in Fermanagh took upon itself to lecture – in the mildest possible way, of course – the local gentry.

In those days of the big house, inhabited by wealthy families many of whom were both landed and titled, and which had grown over the years to be a centre of power and influence in rural communities, such daring was unusually bold. But the local newspaper, the *Impartial Reporter*, was too clever to make a direct attack on its target – 'the cruel and immoral practices of the horse race'. Instead it took a roundabout way of saying what it had to say.

Urging country gentlemen and women who lived on the borders of Lower Lough Erne to follow the example of their fellows who lived on Upper Lough Erne, 'respecting the procurement of yachts and annually exercising their skill in sailing', the newspaper went on: 'Apart from the friendly and convivial occasions that would thus be afforded our gentry and their families for social intercourse, sailing is an innocent amusement … it encourages the art of building vessels most suitable for our waters and gives employment to sailors, while it instructs the peasantry to navigate …'

Although the tone is lofty and even absurd, and the sentiments obsequiously put, the *Impartial Reporter* was merely doing what newspapers have always done – reflecting a current trend which a century and a half later is still going strong.

Lough Erne has a long history in sailing. There are even medieval records referring to a branch of the Maguire family in the thirteenth century who ruled the local waterways and whose coat of arms bears a neat little two-masted sailing boat – proof positive that sailing on the lough does indeed go back a long way. A local bard and poet of the sixteenth century, Timothy O'Higgins, wrote of the bay as 'such a forest of boat masts they conceal the beach and its waves'.

The Maguire connection survived a long time – a family of the name was recorded in 1820 as boat-builders on the upper lake. And today another clan member, Ursula Maguire, is the secretary of the Irish Yachting Association. All round, therefore, the Maguires could be said to have founded the first yacht club in Ireland.

One to hotly dispute that would be the Lough Erne Yacht Club, founded in 1818 and proudly claiming to be the oldest in the world (a claim disputed by others and made by many). Certainly it was running organized races before any other known yacht club.

It had other functions too, or at least the *Impartial Reporter* thought so. One of these was to teach the locals how to sail, although the lough had seen sail for as long as anyone could recall. 'Until the boat races commenced some years ago,' the newspaper observed loftily, 'the peasantry never attempted to sail against the wind; but now it is common to see boats laden with turf, stones, timber, &c, sail with the wind right ahead …'

If sail was common enough in those far-off days, it was not the sail we see today on the lough. The mid-nineteenth century was the heyday of big racing schooners owned by wealthy families. With two or even three masts, acres of billowing sail, huge crews, and iced champagne served on deck to large parties, they were, as one writer has observed pungently, the 'maxi class of the mid-Victorian era'.

One of these, a familiar sight on Lough Erne, was the famous *Egeria*, owned by a man called John Mulholland. She was, by all accounts, a fast and handsome vessel and won all before her at local regattas.

What really brought the modern sailing era to the lough was, however, a technical change in sailing itself. The gaff cutter rig, developed during the Napoleonic wars, was the first rig which allowed a sailing vessel to sail to windward – in other words, to sail even against a headwind by tacking from side to side and zig-zagging forward on her course.

Gaff-rigged cutters became popular in naval circles and were very useful indeed for such work as chasing smugglers and carrying dispatches, both of which needed speedy and easily handled vessels.

Sailing on Upper Lough Erne

In those days around the turn of the eighteenth century, Enniskillen was a major garrison town. As well as the officers in the town, many local gentlemen were also officers of one kind or another. Apart from having this in common, they also knew something about sailing gaff-rigged cutters. In 1815, Lord Belmore,whose family seat was at Castle Coole near Enniskillen, formed the Yacht Club in London with other nautical friends. Later, this was to become the prestigious and mighty Royal Yacht Squadron.

These were moves which spanned a host of developments. People were rich and sporting-minded. Soon the gentry were buying their own boats and racing not only among themselves but also against crack naval racing outfits. These were also the days of big betting on the racecourses of Ascot and Epsom and sailing soon followed suit, with large sums of money changing hands on the outcome of a yacht race. It was said that Lord Belfast had to raise the rents of the hundreds of properties he owned in Belfast to provide him with the funds to build a brig called *Waterwitch*, which he then used to challenge the fast naval craft of the day.

In the early years of the nineteenth century, Enniskillen was yachting mad. Local gentry even advertised in the *Enniskillen Chronicle*, looking for sponsorship for a pleasure-boating map of the lough. By 1820, they were calling themselves 'The Subscribers to the Boat Races on Lough Erne, for the Encouragement of fast Sailing Boats, and for the improvement of the Navigation of the Lake'.

A few short years later 'The Subscribers' had shortened their cumbersome title to something simpler and more succinct: they began to call themselves the Lough Erne Yacht Club, culling their members from all the big houses around the lough, each with their own yachts and trained crews. Thus began the Lough Erne Yacht Club, or the LEYC as it is still known today.

But of all the vessels which have made sailing on Erne what it is today, none are closer to the heart of the true small-boat sailor than the Fairy. Today the Fairy is not just a sailing craft; it is a living and sailing legend.

Fairies have a long history on Erne, to which they are almost unique – they are also raced on Belfast Lough. They began life in the year before Henry Ford built his first Model-T motor car, as small and fast racing yachts which were designed to be bought not by the Big House gentry with plenty of money, but by enthusiasts of more modest means.

Built between 1905 and 1907, they were equipped with what was then the very latest sailing rig, the gunter-lug. Fairies are easily handled and sailed, two factors which made them instantly popular. They are also very durable indeed and although they have now been racing joyously on the lough for well over eighty years, there are actually still eight of the original fleet still sailing. If not quite as good as new, they are in remarkable condition for their age. The comparison may be odious – but just how many Model-Ts are still driving the roads while the Fairies sail merrily away?

The heyday of the Fairies was before the First World War, that idyllic Edwardian period which seems so rose-tinted in recall. But the war called many from the big houses, and many ordinary folk indeed who lived beside the lough, to the trenches, never to return. It was with a feeling of ominous foreboding that the Fairies were placed away carefully on the racks of the Crom boathouse at the end of the 1913 season, forebodings which were well founded. Many of the Fermanagh people who joined the war fell while fighting for king and country. Racing was forgotten.

But not for long. Although the Fairies were never again to reach their former popularity, a few local enthusiasts such as the Tippings and the Richardsons got yacht-racing going again. They started a class for Snipes, another small boat, with an overgrown mast, a villainous centreboard and a tendency to turn on its head if given half a chance – but a wonderful boat to sail.

When another World War intervened, racing slackened, but after the war had ended, Commodore Henry Richardson and Robert Grosvenor, later Duke of Westminster, re-formed the LEYC and threw the doors open for anyone to join. Democracy reigned: the era of the big house and the gentry was fast slipping away, although it was to be the 1960s before Horace Fleming became the first 'non-gentry' commodore.

On almost any day, particularly in the summer months, you can see the Fairies sail. They have regular races, moving along with sedate dignity like superior dowagers amid a litter of all sorts of yachts, including the popular J24. On a Sunday, when people come from all over Ireland to try out Erne's ideal yachting waters, the Fairies are the cynosure of all eyes, proud bearers of a long tradition which goes back as far as the medieval Maguires, through to the Georgian gentlemen, the Subscribers to the Boat Races, the elegant Victorian era and their own memorable Edwardian beginnings.

Period piece: a Fairy on Lough Erne

The Flying Boats

Just after dawn on 26 May 1941, Denis Briggs eased his Catalina flying-boat off the placid waters of Lough Erne, turned westward and flew towards the Atlantic Ocean across the peaceful Irish countryside. Another routine day had begun.

Catalina AH 545 Z of 209 Squadron was accustomed to this sort of work. Briggs was an experienced pilot, one of the many R.A.F. then stationed at Castle Archdale on Lough Erne.

In the dimmish light of an early summer morning, the plane droned on over a corner of Ireland, crossing a landscape where farmers were sleepily getting from their beds to milk their cows and begin a day's work. Now and then the bare grey tips of mountains rose and fell under the wings of the Catalina. In the co-pilot's seat sat Ensign Leonard Smith, one of seven American observers attached to the R.A.F. at Castle Archdale. To his friends he was known as Tuck Smith; and as such he was to go down to posterity.

As the plane slowly chugged its way out over the coast of Ireland and then out over the grey waters of the Atlantic, it was soon full daylight. Both men sat quietly, Briggs concentrating on flying the Catalina which, although a reliable plane, had few of the modern technical improvements which have made flying so much easier. Tuck Smith watched the sea endlessly. He had little else to do: time hung heavily on their hands.

Watching the sea was part of their job. Flights went out daily from Castle Archdale to patrol the Atlantic to the west. First they were looking for German submarines, the dreaded U-boats, and second they were on patrol duty, escorting heavily laden convoys of Allied ships travelling across the Atlantic. In those early years of the war, the U-boats had wreaked a dreadful toll on Allied shipping. 'For the first year of the war,' wrote local Fermanagh historian Breege McCusker, 'Germany was content to attack ships bringing goods coming into Britain … she tried to cut off her lifeline with the rest of the world …'

By the autumn of 1940, a year or so into the war, each German U-boat stationed off the west coast of Ireland was sinking an average of five or six Allied merchant vessels a month – a crippling success rate which owed much of that success to the fact that air cover from America or mainland Britain could not get far enough out in the Atlantic to protect their ships.

Castle Archdale was to change all that. Northern Ireland was, and is, British territory, and by early 1941 R.A.F. Lough Erne had come into being, based at Castle Archdale on Lough Erne. Equipped with Catalinas and Sunderland flying-boats, they had the capacity to fly out over the sea and look after the convoys so desperately needing help. But to do that, they had to fly over the land of the Irish Republic. And the Republic was neutral in the war.

Oxlip meets the Catalina. During the Second World War, these flying boats were stationed on Lough Erne.

Few diplomatic problems have been as ticklish as this one. The English prime minister, Winston Churchill, made plain his feelings at the end of the war towards Irish rejection of his request for the Republic to allow British ships to use Irish ports. 'We left the de Valera Government to frolic with the Germans and later with the Japanese representatives to their heart's content,' said the man who had spent a good deal of his childhood living in Phoenix Park in Dublin.

In a dignified reply, the Irish prime minister, Eamon de Valera, had rejected the charge; by then, few of the public knew that in the early years of the war he had agreed, albeit reluctantly, to allow British flying boats to leave Lough Erne and fly through what became known as the Donegal corridor, across Irish airspace, to protect Allied shipping in the Atlantic.

It was a dangerous game that de Valera played – a neutral country was helping another country at war. It was imperative that the German diplomatic staff stationed in Dublin knew nothing of what was going on; had they known, the Republic might well have been dragged into a war it did not want, could not afford and stood to lose much from.

All this was, however, far from the mind of pilot Denis Briggs and observer Tuck Smith on that 1941 May morning. By 9.30 or so, they were flying over a grey and rough sea, the wind gusting to 40 miles (64km) an hour. Below them, rolling waves and blowing scud made visibility difficult. Grey clouds often enveloped them as they flew along their monotonous course.

At around 9.45, Tuck spotted what he thought was a ship. They came down to about 1,500 feet to have a closer look. 'It was a black shape in the sea,' said Briggs afterwards. They came close enough, about a quarter of a mile away, to be able to identify the ship.

It was the *Bismarck*.

'I was a little surprised to see it,' said Smith after the war, feeling his words carefully.

The Catalina crew had struck gold.

The *Bismarck* was the infamous German battleship which, two days earlier, had engaged the Royal Navy ships the *Hood* and the *Prince of Wales*, in a memorable naval encounter. The *Hood* alone lost 92 officers and 1,400 men in the attack. The *Bismarck* herself had been damaged and was limping towards France for repairs when the Lough Erne Catalina swooped down and recognized her.

Like a cornered animal, the *Bismarck* turned her guns on the Catalina. Briggs said later that there was so much gunfire it was like one big flash. Shots hammered into the hull of the flying-boat, gouging neat holes in the fabric. The crew stuffed the holes with rubber plugs and checked that the fuel tanks had not been hit.

Now was no time for foolish bravado; besides, their orders were to search for and shadow the *Bismarck*. The first object had been accomplished and now it was time for the second. It was imperative to stay in the air and watch the German battleship. Meeting another

Catalina, they managed to get the news back to the authorities that they had sighted the battleship; the next day she was engaged and sunk. Briggs and Smith had made their names a legend.

Or had they? The irony was that Tuck Smith was an American and thus neutral – America had not joined the war at that time and in fact did not do so until after the débâcle at Pearl Harbor. Because he was on a war mission and was neutral, Tuck Smith's role in the sighting of the *Bismarck* had to be kept secret until after the war. Denis Briggs instead got all the credit.

The most senior German officer to survive the sinking of the *Bismarck* was Baron Burkard von Mullenheim-Rechberg, who later wrote a book on the episode. After the war had ended, many years later, Tuck and the Baron whose ship he had helped to sink met up in Chicago. The scars of battle healed by the passage of years, they spent an evening together, reminiscing.

At the end of the night, Baron von Mullenheim leaned towards Smith, patted his arm and said, 'You know, Tuck, I must tell you – you disturbed us very much that day.' And Tuck replied, 'I'm glad we did – you were disturbing us very much!'

If the sighting and subsequent sinking of the *Bismarck* was the highlight of the R.A.F. 'occupation' of Lough Erne during the war years, there were other, lesser-known but just as apocalyptic events on a smaller and local scale. This was hardly surprising, given that a peaceful, rural area, remote from all the stresses and strains of war and its attendant miseries, had suddenly been pitchforked into having its houses commandeered as housing for hundreds of pilots, engineers, observers and so on, having its towns and villages filled with the trappings of war – and, perhaps most disturbing of all, its local girls becoming enraptured by the glitz and glamour of Americans whose life they had known only from movies.

For six years, Lough Erne was the base of Coastal Command, with its legions of Catalinas and Sunderlands landing and taking off from the waters of the lough; home for hundreds of airmen of all sorts; home to the hum and drone of aircraft engines, the comings-and-goings of a nation at war. For a people whose quiet lives revolved around farming and the monthly fair day, the arrival of the R.A.F. and later on of the Americans was a cataclysmic event, one which was to affect their lives in many ways and for many years – in some cases, for the rest of their lives.

It is a fascinating story. The disasters were many. Flying-boats then were not the safest of craft, and neither was Lough Erne very safe either to take off from or to land on. Much of it was shallow, and rocks were never very far from the surface.

It rained a lot—there are records of Americans in particular bemoaning the fact that the sun never shone on Fermanagh! – and visibility could be so bad that planes could neither land nor take off. The Donegal corridor, through which the planes had to fly to and from the Atlantic, was riddled with deceptive hills and valleys. There were crashes aplenty, some of them fatal. As Breege McCusker wrote, 'The north-west coast was to be a burial ground for many airmen and the remains of Catalinas and Sunderlands can still be found on the boggy slopes of the Donegal, Sligo and Leitrim mountains.'

If there were disasters, there were successes too, There was the momentous occasion of the *Bismarck* but there were also other, less dramatic successes, like the sinking of several U-boats. As the war progressed, slowly but surely the men from Castle Archdale, flying out doggedly each day to patrol the grey waters of the Atlantic, began to gain the upper hand over the U-boats. They had been given a job to do and they did it well.

In between these disasters and successes, life went on as it will. On the ground, both the British and the Americans, who came in numbers to Lough Erne after America had entered the war, became not just a community in themselves but mixed and matched with the local communities in a thousand different ways. They brought a new, exciting and varied life to the peaceful rural community in which they found themselves.

War was in the air and with it a sort of reckless romance; no one knew what might happen, how long they might live. So life was lived to the fullest by local and foreigner alike. Not a few local girls married their peaceful invaders – much to the chagrin of the local lads!

When the war ended, airmen left, as suddenly as they had appeared. The flying-boats were quietly scuttled, the vast hangars abandoned, the big houses returned to their owners, the other 'occupied' houses deserted by the airmen. Today, sailing yachts use the giant slipways which once were used to haul flying-boats from the water as launching-pads for their own form of transport.

Now the placid waters of the lough and the farmhouses clustered around its shores hear only the hiss of racing bow-waves, the clatter of sheet and sail. The flying-boats have gone and with them the gallant men who flew them. But the memories, as they will, linger on.

Catalina over Fermanagh. During the war, many were wrecked on the surrounding hills.

Figures of Stone

*Then I found a two-faced stone
On burial ground,
God-eyed, sex-mouthed, its brain
A watery wound …*

White Island figures

In the poet's way, as in no other, Seamus Heaney encapsulates the inscrutable and mysterious strangeness of one of the most remarkable aspects of Lough Erne – the stone carvings which, like beacons of a long-lost and forgotten history, bedeck the countryside of County Fermanagh.

Ireland has a history of stone carving. But nowhere in the entire island is there the richness and strangeness of those around Lough Erne. Here is a unique heritage of stone figures and heads; what one historian called the carvers' 'veneration of the human head' crops up everywhere in images which are at the same time compelling and repellent, glaze-eyed idols of a millennium long vanished.

All of this is hardly out of place in a part of the country where legend and everyday life intermix. Not for nothing are the unique sailing craft which race on Lough Erne known as Fairies, for this is the land of the Little People. There is the story told, for instance, of the old woman who was asked by her priest if she believed in the 'Little People'. 'Indeed and I don't,' she retorted, 'but shure, they do have the life pestered out of me, all the same.'

But who and what and why are these stone figures, these mesmeric and inscrutable faces forever gazing from blank eyes? No one knows for certain, other than to confirm their ancient lineage. Are they Christian? Pagan? Or some unknown age, race or creed?

On Boa Island, in the ancient graveyard at Caldragh, stand what are perhaps the most famous and intriguing of all the stone figures – the Janiform (two-faced) idols, two figures set back to back, arms crossed, with large heads, pointed chins, each with what appears to be a beard. They have a curiously compelling quality, challenging the viewer to find out more about them.

The Boa Island figures have excited all sorts of learned comment over the years. The consensus now is that they are pre-Christian, at the very least with a pagan influence.

But why so many stone heads? As with so much that is Irish, the answer lies somewhere with the Celts, those first millennium BC tribes from Central Europe who used metal tools and weapons and made their reputation as great traders. The head is perhaps the most important religious symbol in the Celtic culture, much as is the cross in Christian culture. Bronze Age Europeans used the head as a symbol of the sun.

But there is another, more sombre cult – the reverence for severed human heads. Severed heads are a familiar theme in Ireland – many Irish sagas relate how heroes and victors in battle returned to their tribes bearing the heads of their slain enemies. One theory is that the heads were venerated because they were thought to contain the human spirit after death and that possession of the head prolonged the triumph of the slayer. Fermanagh indeed has itself its share of such tales – a twelfth-century chieftain's head was carried away by his killers and kept for a month, while a sixteenth-century chieftain, one of the Maguires, adorned the posts of his garden with no fewer than sixteen severed heads.

And the Boa Island two-faced figures? They are undoubtedly cult idols but their origins are very vague indeed. Most scholars liken them to the Celtic figures found on the continent; the double figure, it is said, could also reflect the Celtic belief in the power of twins, who were believed to enjoy divine protection, or could stem from the primitive belief that to have two faces was in some way increasing the power of the idol.

We are on more certain historical ground on another Lough Erne island, White Island. Here are six statues, all carved with great skill and artistry and all it is thought, carved between the ninth and eleventh centuries. They are easy – some of them at least – to identify: a portrait of Christ in triumph, two referring directly to the New Testament, one probably of Christ or St Anthony, another of King David. The sixth is the odd man – or woman – out, a strange, lewd, grinning, female figure.

The White Island statues, say historians, are not actual portraits of dead people but instead are meant to convey spiritual meanings and ideas. They are also believed to have served as caryatids, or figures which held something upon them such as an altar. Whatever their function, whatever their origins, these and other stone figures and heads from the region provide a series of extraordinary images in these modern days of technology where few secrets are ever real secrets. That elusiveness – the feeling that we will never know from whence or why they came – is part of their compelling and distinctive charm.

A Place of Pilgrimage

Every year, thousands of people make their diverse ways to a remote lake in Donegal, get into a boat and arrive on an island in the middle of the lake. For three days and nights they eat just one meal every twenty-four hours, a plain meal of dry bread or toast, black tea or coffee, or even just water. They take off their shoes and walk barefoot on sharp stones. For twenty-four hours, they don't sleep. And all the time they pray.

This is not a vision of medieval Europe, a recollection of penitent times, a relic of the Middle Ages. This is today, the twentieth century, when humankind has been to the Moon and back, shops by pressing computer keys and gets money from a hole in the wall.

We are in Lough Derg, place of pilgrimage.

Strangely enough, pilgrimages are back in fashion. Ireland has many, some of them known the world over. Croagh Patrick is one, Lough Derg another.

'To the outsider,' writes historian Laurence Flynn, 'it may well seem a strange and uninviting ritual, complex, outmoded perhaps – even medieval. If it needs apologia, there are two that may be offered. Firstly, from the Christian point of view, the exercises centre on the sacramental celebrations … secondly, almost 30,000 people each year find some of that peace with themselves, with their neighbour and with their God which is the goal of so much human searching …'

Lough Derg lies a few miles from the village of Pettigo in Donegal. That a place of religious and peaceful pilgrimage like Lough Derg should be neighbour to a village which is unique in Ireland in that half of it is in the Republic and half in Northern Ireland, with a division marked by an ugly wall of wire and concrete, is in itself something of an irony.

St Patrick's Purgatory, as the place of pilgrimage is known, is situated on Station Island, a two-acre island and one of about twenty on the lake. The name itself is revealing – it comes from the Latin *statio*, meaning a post of duty. The word and its attendant associations are not confined to Lough Derg: all over rural Ireland, the Catholic practice still exists of having Mass said in an individual's private house every so often. It's called doing the stations. On Lough Derg, station denotes a pattern of prayers which are performed around the circles of low stone walls on the island, known as penitential beds.

Why is this small island, its every inch built up with buildings, walls, paths, known as St Patrick's Purgatory? The place has been one of pilgrimage since the twelfth century – it was, oddly enough, the only Irish landmark on some renaissance maps. A historian has written: 'St Patrick's Purgatory was the medieval rumour which terrified travellers, awed the greatest of criminals, attracted the boldest of knight errantry, puzzled the theologian, englamoured Ireland, haunted Europe, influenced the current views and doctrines of purgatory, and not least inspired Dante.'

The association of the island with St Patrick, patron saint of Ireland, goes back a long way. Even the name of the lough, Derg, is said to come from the Gaelic word for red, *dearg*, believed to be derived from the blood of the serpent which Patrick is thought to have slain here. It could also mean cave (*deirc*), as indeed a cave is shown on ancient maps.

It is this cave which probably gives the island its name of St Patrick's Purgatory. Certainly in the old days pilgrims spent long periods of time in the cave. It was customary in those days to spend not three days on the island, as now, doing penance, but fifteen days. And one whole day was spent in what was called the Hole – the cave. One pilgrim, known as the Knight Owein, engendered a horrific tale of hell on earth after he had spent some time in the cave – he reported visions of souls tormented by devils with white-hot nails and cauldrons of boiling metal before he crossed a treacherous bridge and emerged safely into paradise. This tale is said to have inspired Dante's *Inferno*.

Today, however, those tales are mere legend for the 30,000 pilgrims who come here to fast, keep a vigil, say their prayers and celebrate a series of ancient Christian sacramental rites in a process which has changed very little for 400 years or so. They are the perpetuators of an ancient and honoured tradition, a visible testament to the strength of religious conviction which has doggedly kept the island a place of pilgrimage down through centuries of repression, vandalism, destruction, disbelief. The place has been closed down, sacked, its buildings levelled. Yet throughout the years of persecution, principally from the sixteenth century onwards, pilgrims secretly and tirelessly kept the practice up.

In a world increasingly committed to the worship of the material, Lough Derg stands out as a survival of ancient and symbolic penitential pilgrimage. Curiously enough, the people who go there are not all old, or making their final peace before going to their maker. Instead, more and more young people are coming – symbolic in themselves perhaps of a return to the religious beliefs which have kept this ancient place of pilgrimage alive for so long.

Devenish Island on Lough Erne

Traveller of the Seas

An eel fisher on the Erne

It's called *Anguilla anguilla* and most people have a strong revulsion for it. Its life history is so far removed from the normal that in olden days people thought it was formed from a mixture of horsehair and mud. Even today, though its flesh is a delicacy, little enough is known about the freshwater eel.

Eels are odd creatures. For what other species would take it into its head, once autumn is here, to leave its freshwater home and travel with single-minded determination some 3,000 miles (4800km) far out into the glassy depths of the Sargasso Sea, there to spawn and die?

Scientists only discovered this bizarre sequence of life when they found that the *Leptocephalus,* which had been thought to be a species in its own right living in the Atlantic plankton chain, all of a sudden one day became an elver (a young eel) and later an adult eel. Thus was the horsehair-and-mud legend de-mystified.

Ireland is a country of eels. Every angler who has fished seriously for almost any species of fish in our freshwater lakes and rivers and ponds will have come into slimy contact with an eel at some time. They grow large and live long; there is a verified case of a small lake in County Meath where two gigantic eels were poisoned and taken ashore. One was 12 feet (3.6m) long and weighed 41 lb (18.45kg), the other was 10 feet (3m) long and weighed 29 lb (13.05kg) (it should be noted that the record rod-caught Irish eel is about 7 lb/3.15kg).

An eel's age can be determined through a simple process, and there is a recent record of an eel in the west of Ireland which was twenty-nine years old – and others have been recorded which were considerably older.

Juvenile eels leave the Sargasso Sea spawning grounds in the Atlantic and enter rivers in spring. Once ensconced in their new freshwater homes, they can stay for twenty years or even longer before they migrate back to sea, there to spawn and die. They live by catching and eating invertebrates and also feed on any waste matter – a habit which to some extent accounts for the revulsion in which they are generally held! They are ferocious predators, particularly of small fish such as young trout and salmon, minnow, gudgeon and so on.

Remarkably little research has been done into eels in Ireland – most of it by that fine fisheries scientist, Christopher Moriarty – but commercial fishing for eels is much more developed. The Electricity Supply Board, which controls the River Shannon and its myriad associated rivers and lakes, is building up a large commercial eel fishery. There is a long tradition of eel-fishing on the bigger Shannon lakes, where the tradition (and the rights) have been handed down through family generations, but nowhere is eel-fishing more famous than in Northern Ireland, where Lough Neagh (and to a lesser extent Lough Erne) is a mecca for the commercial catching of eels.

Eels are trapped by nets at certain times when they are 'on the move' – that is in late spring when they appear to become much more active after the chills of winter, and again in the autumn, when migration takes place. The nets are placed strategically at points where eels collect in large numbers, such as weirs, locks and so on. In rivers, the current is sometimes diverted to channel migrating eels downstream into large conical nets and from there into well-aerated holding tanks, where the eels are held. The best time for catching eels is, curiously enough, at night – and there seems to be little real truth in the old adage that eels sometimes travel by land from river to river as they migrate. Eels can live a long time out of water but are not amphibious!

Irish tastes have been slow to take to the eel; quite why this is no one knows but there are plenty of theories. One is that the natural if superstitious fear of the eel being somehow related to the snake has put people off eating it. But things are very different elsewhere. There is a huge continental market, particularly for smoked eel, which is esteemed a rare delicacy and commands very high prices indeed. There is now a thriving and growing eel market between Ireland and mainland European countries, and even further afield to such places as America and Japan. In recent years this has made the eel a valuable resource, but there is a problem in managing that resource.

So little is known about the eel population in Ireland, its size, distribution and ability to renew itself, that scientists and conservationists are already voicing concern as to its future. There now seems little doubt that the eel is increasingly being regarded as a valuable freshwater resource in a commercial sense. This will continue to pose problems. Because we know so little about eels in Ireland, more must be known before wholesale commercial exploitation can be given free rein. That much surely is owed to this strange and mysterious creature, a thing of myth and legend.

Chapter 6

Back on the water, I head *Oxlip* west, towards the edge of the world.

After Boa Island and Lough Derg I am living in the past. I am inside the skin of a pilgrim from central Europe who travelled by boat along this lake 1,000 years ago. At night he sleeps on islands, listening to wolves howling across the water. By day he slips along close to the shore, lowering sail occasionally when he sees another craft – it might be a pirate and he is, quite literally, keeping a low profile. And all the time, as he penetrates further west, deeper into the wilderness, is the throbbing fear that he will sail off the edge of the world. What courage to keep going, what faith in God.

I am in the fifth week of the journey and may be losing some grip on reality. So I decide to go for a walk in a garden.

A garden is like a cage of circus lions. It is nature with its teeth pulled, forced to obey the will of man or, rather more commonly, of woman. Despite this, I love gardens and spend a lot of time in my own. I find them soothing and sane. Just the job when you're a little tired and becoming obsessed by history and archaeology.

The ultimate gardens were made by the Elizabethans. Tully Castle is an Elizabethan fortified manor on the shore of the lake. It was a 'plantation castle', granted to a loyal subject of the Queen on condition that he kept the natives restrained. It's now a carefully preserved ruin, and the natives are as unrestrained as ever. But the authorities who look after this sort of thing round here have re-created an Elizabethan garden in the castle bawn or yard.

Tully Castle, with its restored Elizabethan garden

Books and television both fall down when it comes to the question of smell. This is a pity, because the first thing I find is a scent garden. Here's sweet bay, lovage, thyme, rosemary and rue … and several things with names I can't remember but with delicious smells when you crush a leaf.

Low hedges of trimmed box and fences of wattle guide me round a strictly geometrical walk, past beds of marigolds and pansies. Now it's more colour than scent – and a certain earthy practicality because most of the plants are edible. The Elizabethans used marigold petals and the violas in their 'sallets'. By this stage I've given up trying to put names on the plants in English and Latin. Taxonomy is a boring game that gets in the way of enjoyment. What is this strange conceit that believes we have to be able to label something beautiful? Isn't it another manifestation of our neurotic craving to get the better of nature? Eschew the Sin of Nomenclature, Dick, and enjoy the garden.

Feeling better, I steam off to another plantation castle.

Castle Caldwell is not at all like Tully Castle. The ruin and its demesne are owned by the Royal Society for the Protection of Birds – and they have their own agenda when it comes to the relationship between human beings and nature.

There has been no attempt to restore the gardens and they have almost disappeared. Almost but not quite. I am interested in trees and find some striking and exotic specimens growing among the native timber around the ruin. Here is what I think must be the largest and finest field maple in Ireland … an imported tree. And here the Sin of Nomenclature catches me again – here is a tree I can't identify. I pull off a spray of leaves so I can take it home and look it up in a reference book. But it's a warm day. The leaves soon wither, the spray disintegrates and I lose interest and abandon it.

The building itself is a riotous example of *sic transit gloria mundi*. Ferns, ash plants and elder bushes are devouring the masonry, thrusting through empty windows and recycling the mortar holding together a hodge-podge of several centuries of architecture. I spend some time walking through the empty halls, admiring the vegetation. I like the place.

Outside there are a number of paths wandering through the trees. I take one to an odd-looking wooden cabin perched on the edge of the lake and discover something even more soothing than an Elizabethan garden. It's a bird-watching hide. I sit on a wooden bench with a sneaky slit-window open and my trusty Nikon miniature binoculars at my eyes … for several hours.

The private lives of waterbirds are fascinating. A great crested grebe, a male I think, is doing a lot of diving and coming up with something, fish I think, in its beak. It waits until its got about half a dozen and then a fat, fluffy, adolescent chick, striped in pale and dark brown, comes over to be fed. And I've discovered another grebe, a female I think, dozing on a floating nest of dead sedges. Is daddy feeding the only survivor of the first clutch while she incubates a second?

A Great Crested Grebe, one of the many waterbirds which can still be seen on the waterway

Then, great excitement, a flock of eight dark ducks of a species I can't identify flights in. And there's a coot climbing up a log that sticks out of the water and revealing the most ridiculous pair of over-sized feet. And a waterhen with a nervous tic in its tail and a mute swan looking very elegant until it gets hungry and starts to graze on the lake bottom like an upside-down giraffe.

I sit in my dark cabin, a Peeping Tom prying into the lives of creatures of another species. Nobody knows I'm here, nobody knows what I'm doing, and I'm getting secret pleasure out of it. Why do I feel slightly guilty? Maybe it's that Protestant background. I'd better get back to the boat. I've been here for hours.

Oxlip is a little temperamental today. Running a steamboat is a balancing act. You get a good fire going and plenty of water in the boiler and eventually you wait and she builds up a head of steam. This is the moment to leave. But there's a delay … usually caused by the television crew that's following us around. So she blows off the steam through the safety valve and the pressure needle starts to drop. Then we get the call to action. We limp on at three-quarter speed, conserving our resources. But we're running short of water. We have to use steam pressure to get water into the boiler and the level drops very close to the danger point. And the fire is getting lower. We put fuel in, but the immediate result before the briquettes catch is to blacken the fire and lower the temperature. We're on a downward spiral which will end with us having to stop and let the boat drift for twenty minutes while we get everything in balance again. Well, it's a challenge.

Eventually the lake becomes a river and pushes westwards for the Atlantic. It doesn't do so decisively. It gradually develops a series of lagoons which are full of eel nets and joined by complicated channels. Then it's properly a river at last, with quite a strong current which draws *Oxlip* under a concrete bridge. One span of the bridge has been blown off by explosives and Her Majesty's sappers have carried out a makeshift wooden repair. What a strange country this is. Another mile and a cluster of buildings appears round a bend.

Belleek is a border town – though 90 per cent of it is in the North. It's world-famous for parian china – a thin, off-white porcelain which, all too often, is decorated with small green shamrocks. The forecourt of the factory is full of tour buses. The world seems to love Belleek china. I'm sorry but I don't.

Belleek is a town with a fine street with its back to the water. So many Irish towns seem to be slightly ashamed to have a river running through. It's something to be left at the bottom of the back garden where, perhaps, once upon a time, the outside toilet used to discharge its unmentionable effluent into the water. The river? ... we don't talk about things like that, dear ... It's not very polite.

Thankfully attitudes are changing. The townspeople have discovered money floating on the river in the form of Germans and Italians in hire cruisers. And this new waterway has been opened which links the Erne to the Shannon ... where there are even more hire cruisers filled with Germans and Italians with wallets. So, behind the unpainted back walls of the houses, down at the bottom of the long back gardens, they have built a marina. It's still rather new-looking, though nicely done. And *Oxlip* will have to wait here for a little while, nudging her white fenders against a new jetty. Because this is the present limit of downstream navigation. The place where a boat journey ends.

Rogan's of Ballyshannon, where fishing flies have been tied since 1830

All Rogan's flies are tied by hand, as they have been for almost two centuries

But I can't stop here. We're only a few miles from the Atlantic and the river mouth and I have to see the thing through to its conclusion.

Ballyshannon in County Donegal is the place where the Erne meets the tide. And it may owe its name to Giraldus Cambrensis and his premature belief that this was actually the second mouth of the Shannon. It's a town I've always liked; it climbs up a hill and looks down on a pretty estuary with small islands, which broadens into sandy shallows and then throws up a bar to keep the Atlantic rollers out. There is a rather menacing dam of grey concrete which broods in the background and makes electricity. It's the reason I had to leave *Oxlip* behind. But Ballyshannon has a cut-stone integrity about its architecture and its people which overcomes the slight embarrassment of the dam.

It's also a legendary mecca in the world of flyfishing. I have to go to the old bridge and pay homage to a billboard on a gable-end which proclaims that Rogan of Ballyshannon have been tying fishing flies uninterruptedly since 1830. Built-wing salmon flies, poems in coloured feather, are an Irish invention. They were developed in the nineteenth century by artist-craftsmen in the two great centres of Castleconnell and Ballyshannon. We rapidly lost our market lead. Most fishing flies in the world today are tied in Kenya, where female labour is very cheap. But as I walk around the corner, off the bridge, I discover something rather wonderful. There, sitting in a window like old-style village tailors, are two women tying flies. But the strange thing is that they are doing it in the nineteenth-century way: the hook is held in their fingers, not in a vice, the hackles are wound by hand, not with pliers … in fact, the only tools they are using are a small pair of scissors each. Why are they doing it this way? Why are they not allowed the luxury of the simple tools their sisters in Kenya use? The answer is that the Rogans believe in quality and they believe that the old way produces a better fly. I walk away hoping that a world that is tiresomely full of fast-food franchises, disposable cigarette lighters and paper tissue can continue to support those two women in the window in Ballyshannon.

I stroll down towards the sea. I am back in the Republic again and I think about this border business. I am a Protestant married to a Catholic with two children who are Irish more than anything else. When they grow older I don't think they'll have the patience to tolerate all this nonsense. They'll laugh at the Sin of Nomenclature which sticks labels on plants and animals and Catholics and Protestants and Unionists and Republicans. And, like all children everywhere who laugh at their parents, they'll be right.

The Atlantic surf is crashing on the bar at the end of the estuary. And beyond is a blue emptiness stretching to America. The journey is over. A journey's end is like a little death. I am glad to be relieved of the discomfort, the worry and the occasional fear of it all. But really I don't want it to stop. I want to travel for ever. *DW*

Under way

Rogan's of Ballyshannon

"If you were to ask present-day fly fishermen to quote you the names of famous Irish fly-makers of the nineteenth century, I would guess that, unhesitatingly, they would reply – Rogan …'

Thus writes E.J. Malone, author of the definitive book on Irish fishing flies and their makers, *Irish Trout and Salmon Flies*, a book which delves deeply into the mysterious world of the fishing fly – mysterious, that is, to anyone other than a fly-fisher.

A fly-fisher, to define it clearly, is one who casts an artificial fly, usually an imitation of natural flies which are on or about water, in the hope of deceiving or enticing a fish into taking the fly, becoming hooked and eventually landed. Like all sports, it too can become an obsession, not least in that its detail rather than its broad philosophy is what excites the fanatic.

Artificial flies lend themselves to such fanaticism and obsessiveness. Their very names are redolent of romance and mystery – the Alexandra, the Black and Silver Spider, the Gold-Ribbed Hare's Ear, the Grouse and Orange, the Claret Bumble. What can they mean, these strange and esoteric names? To the angler, of course, they mean all – the ways and means by which he or she can find the way to a fish's heart. And stomach.

Tying flies is a skill like any other. Although many anglers like to tie their own flies, finding that catching a fish on a fly they have tied themselves lends an extra and pleasurable dimension to their angling, most anglers rely on shop-bought or specially ordered flies for their essential equipment.

In Ireland, particularly, there is a long, distinguished and even noble tradition of fly-tying. Many of the great flies of angling have been created in Ireland by Irish fly-tyers. There is a tradition at least a couple of centuries old, beginning with the great names of Gorman of County Clare and Hynes of County Galway. But perhaps the most influential name of all, though little known to many anglers, is that of one Thomas Ettingsall, who advocated the use and dressing of the dry-fly (i.e. a fly that floats on top of the surface rather than sinking beneath it, as with the wet fly) long before many more famous names had risen to prominence and had been given, erroneously, the credit for inventing the dry-fly.

One name, however, will certainly be mentioned by any Irish fly-fisher who knows anything at all about the sport—and that is the name of Rogan. Rogan's shop, established in 1830, is still going strong in the Donegal seaside town of Ballyshannon. And perhaps no greater tribute could be paid either to its longevity or pre-eminence than by the fishing author Donald Overfield, who in his definitive *Famous Flies and their Originators*, wrote:

'A book about the artificial fly that did not contain a chapter about the craft of dressing as practised in Ireland would be roast beef without horseradish sauce. Who better to represent that country than Michael Rogan, a man who became a legend in his own time and one who was to found a dynasty that has lasted, unbroken, for the best part of one hundred and forty years, years during which the name Rogan has come to be allied with the best in salmon fly design and construction and that of the trout fly.'

It was a Michael Rogan too who first brought the family to wider fame than the locality of Donegal. Born in 1833, he learned the art from his father and within a few short years had achieved an enviable reputation for his skill. His great flies, those which have lasted until now and which will withstand the tests of time and technology, are the Green Parson, Rogan's Fancy and the Ballyshannon.

Ironically, however, he is probably best known – erroneously – as the inventor of the famous fly, the Fiery Brown. Rogan did not actually invent the pattern, but what he did do was to dress it with specially-dyed materials which gave it a brilliance and lustre hitherto unequalled, thus making the fly a much, much better one than previously.

What is true, however, is the story that to achieve the brilliant and enduring colours of his materials, he steeped them in a barrel of either horse's or donkey's urine which he kept in the rear of his premises, until the smell became so bad that the sanitary authorities had to intervene!

One of his greatest innovations, and one which has also lasted to this day, is his method of tying wings on salmon flies in such a way that when the fly is pulled through the water while being fished, each individual fibre reacts against the water's pull in a different way, imbuing the fly with a brilliant translucency which is amazingly lifelike and attractive – or at least the fish think so!

Another peculiarity of Rogan flies is that they are not only all dressed by hand (many flies these days are dressed by machine and made in Africa) but the tyers use no artificial tools at all, other than a pair of scissors. To anyone who has tied a fly, using the complicated paraphernalia of fly-tying vice, tweezers, dubbing needle, etc., the thought of having to do without these implements is anathema – and tying even tiny flies a fraction of an inch long with the fingers only seems close to a miracle. Yet that is the way that Rogan's have always tied flies and continue to tie them to this day.

In any family business which has existed for so long, inevitably there are traditions, legends, tall tales. One which the Rogans liked to tell was the story of two Irish Navy officers who were both in love with the same girl and wished to marry her. So they had a bet with each other as to which one of them the girl would marry – and the bet was an unusual one, three dozen ordinary-size salmon flies against one large one. According to Michael Rogan, 'So when she said she'd marry one of them, the other had to ask me to make a Jock Scott (a type of salmon fly) two feet, six inches long.'

The monstrous hook was forged in a Derry foundry and the consumption of precious

The late Michael Rogan, one of the great fly-tiers of his generation

silk and feather was outrageous. When it came to the black hackle, it needed most of a pony's tail; and for the topping, properly the brilliant gold of a golden pheasant's crest, there was nothing to be had that colour and size so he took two long brown golden pheasant tails and dyed them yellow in picric acid. The whole contraption weighed about two and half pounds and, said Michael Rogan, 'tis the only Rogan fly that will never have a chance of catching a fish!'

Another lovely tale concerns Michael Rogan Senior, the founding father of the dynastic business. Like many Donegal people, Michael Rogan was a proud and independent man who bowed the knee to no one. One day he was visited in his shop by an English gentleman of distinguished title. A gentleman himself, Michael courteously offered his guest a pull from his long clay pipe – an old and generous Irish custom. Before putting the pipe in his mouth, however, the visitor fastidiously wiped the stem with a silk handkerchief, and then returned the pipe to Rogan. Not to be outdone, Michael Rogan promptly broke the mouthpiece off the pipe and smoked the shortened stem for the remainder of the distinguished guest's visit.

Winner of countless awards and medals at fisheries exhibitions and shows, the Rogans have handed down the family tradition of their Ballyshannon premises for generation after generation. A mecca for fly-fishers and fly-tyers, and with a thriving export trade all over the world to those discerning anglers who value real quality, the premises is today under new management; but the Rogan tradition lives on in its pursuit of ancient, handcrafted skills – skills which have produced flies which hopefully will continue to catch fish for many years to come.

An Elizabethan Garden

When historians call the Elizabethan period the flowering of English genius, the word 'flowering' takes on a wider meaning. In these islands at least, under the tough thumb of Elizabeth I (1558–1603), began the modern craze for gardening.

Mankind has always gardened in some way or another. For what is gardening but a diversification of crop cultivation? But not until the medieval period had come and gone, and England had begun to create an empire on which the sun never set, did the concept take hold of gardening as a recreation. To coin a pun, it was in the age of Elizabeth that the garden, as it were, came to fruition.

There is a variety of reasons for this development. The main one, however, is that there had arisen in England a system or class of people who were much more privileged than the man-in-the-street. The lineage of royalty was extending fast and being added to by an ever-widening list of titled families, landed gentry and just plain adventurers who had become respectable.

All these people had several things in common – they had money, position, property and time on their hands. Much of this was spent in building ever grander new houses and on beautifying both the houses and the grounds they stood in – a relatively new concept and the forerunner of today's suburban plot by the front door.

In those days, gardening was of course and of necessity very different to what it is today. For one thing, the range of plants, shrubs and trees was tiny compared to today. Cultivation in the sense of propagating plants for gardeners was more or less unknown. But Elizabethan culture was a wide one, encompassing not just material possessions but the arts and culture generally, an era in which prospered music, poetry, painting. It was inevitable therefore that the broadening of the cultural vein should widen still further to take in gardening as an aesthetic movement, something which like music and the arts in general adorned one's life.

If these were influences in the creation of the Elizabethan garden, there were others too. Cookery had also become something of a flowering art: England's huge empire, encompassing several continents and controlling most of the oceans of the world, had provided her explorers and the adventurers who followed on their coat-tails with a whole range of foreign experiences, not the least of which was sampling foreign foods and flavourings. Herbs, spices, condiments of all sorts were being brought back. And this spread also to encouraging a wider use of herbs in cooking – the traditional herbs on which much of the medicine of those and older times was based.

Herbs are central to the Elizabethan garden. It was an age when herbal medicine was much more advanced than any other branch of medical science. Doctors were few and far between and few people had ever seen one, let alone attended one. Distances were vast, transport more or less non-existent and certainly time-consuming. People in general were forced to rely on traditional ways of curing, of which herbal medicine was easily the most popular.

It was a natural development, therefore, that as the fashion for fine houses and estates grew, and with it the passion for gardening which has continued to this day, the Elizabethans formed gardens of herbs, to which were added the few flowers which were then cultivated, such as marigolds, a real Elizabethan favourite, and of course the range of violas and pansies. The herbs were mostly thyme, bay, rosemary, rue. To contain them, and also to prettify their surroundings, small hedges of box were planted, trimmed low to allow the sun to reach the herbs. From this plain base grew the rectangular, low-profiled Elizabethan garden of a small range of flowers and a wider range of herbs. Often the gardens were surrounded by a stone or brick wall or even by a wattle fence. It is a pattern which finds a direct reflection in the dimensions and shapes of many a suburban garden today.

Even to this day, many English gardens are based on Elizabethan principles. The wonderful garden, or series of small gardens, at Sissinghurst in Kent, home of Vita Sackville West, is in reality a series of Elizabethan-type gardens, enhanced by the mellow rose-red of ancient brick which was also used by the Elizabethans. But very few original Elizabethan gardens survive anywhere.

On the shores of Lower Lough Erne lies Tully Castle. It was once the home of John Hume (no, not that John Hume), one of the thousands of settlers who, encouraged by Elizabeth, settled in Ireland in the sixteenth century and obtained large grants of land. Sir John Hume built the house in 1613, ten years after Elizabeth had died. It is a typical fortified tower house of large dimensions; once it had a thatched roof but in 1641 it was burned down by the local Gaelic clan, the Maguires, and was never lived in again. Today it has been restored, but not reroofed, by the Department of the Environment.

So far this is an ordinary enough story; but in a most imaginative move, the Environment Service has re-created alongside the castle a replica of an original Elizabethan garden. Here, between walls of wattle, and sheltered in regimented rectangles by low hedges of trimmed box, are the herbs and flowers which are so characteristic of the sixteenth century.

It is an unreal experience to walk around this small garden, inhaling the explicit smells and scents, crushing the leaves of the herbs as you go (but don't, please, crush too many!). Towards the lake the noble ruin of the castle rises majestically, its tall, gaunt walls seeming almost as if they still house the family which once would have wandered through such a garden. It is an experience which should not be missed.

On the Wing

There are few places in the island of Ireland where bird life is more prolific and undisturbed than in the basin of Lough Erne. That much is obvious to the visitor who, nosing a cruiser gently up the myriad of waterways – rivers, canals, lakes – is surrounded by birds of all shapes, sizes and species. And not just those birds which are attracted to water, for this is a region rich in all types, many of them scarce not only in Ireland but in Europe.

Just a few facts bear out this richness and diversity of bird life. Take a marine duck like the common scoter, which uses the lough as its main breeding ground in these islands. The rare blackcap is nationally important here, as is the even rarer garden warbler – over 15 per cent of all the garden warblers in the whole of Ireland are found in the Crom wildlife park alone, and the lough basin has probably got about half the entire population of this secretive bird in Ireland.

In the same estate, on Inishfendra Island, is the largest colony of herons in Ireland – about seventy nests in all. The loughs, both upper and lower, are nationally important centres for the great crested grebe. And then there are the rare water rails, first cousins of the now almost-extinct corncrake, once such a common bird throughout the countryside.

Why is the basin so rich in bird life? There are plenty of theories and little real scientific evidence. Probably the most persuasive argument is that this is a part of Fermanagh which for many obvious reasons has been left largely to itself, a lucky intervention of providence when added to the many islands which dot the waterways and which afford bird life the sort of seclusion and privacy in which it thrives.

There are other advantages. There are plenty of wetlands in the basin, plenty of water, plenty of woodland. The many islands mean that birds are disturbed only rarely. There is a small human population, which means that the birds are disturbed even less by human activity. Reed swamps are plentiful, while the fen grassland is difficult and expensive for the farmer to drain. In addition, there is now the growing influence of the European Union, which now ordains that much of the basin has been designated as an area of special scientific interest (ASSI)

All of this brings a rich diversity. Sandwich terns, which feed at sea, come all the way to Lough Erne to nest on the islands. The long-eared owls breed on Inishfendra Island, where the huge heronry is also situated. Snipe,curlew, redshank and other waders are thick in the water here, for the Erne basin is one of the top three areas in Ireland for breeding waders. The 650 acres of oak forest, the biggest in Northern Ireland and the third largest area of oak in the whole island, bring such species as the blackcap and garden warbler. The large areas of conifers dotted around the basin yield such species as jays, sparrowhawks and crossbills, while the alder growth which now fringes much of the lough is important for such species as siskin and lesser redpolls.

Besides woodland, the land around the lough is also parkland and farmland, ideal ground for skylarks and meadow pipits, though there is some concern about numbers of these birds, while there are plenty of common birds such as mistle thrushes and so on. Whooper swans and white-fronted geese feed on some of the grasslands, while the wet areas provide suitable habitat for lapwing, redshank, curlew and snipe. There are also some visitors, such as sedge warblers and others.

Areas rich in water are usually also rich in bird life, but the basin does not always reflect this. There is concern about water quality, as in recent years the lough and its rivers and feeder streams have become more and more organically rich from the constant inflow of agricultural fertilizers – a problem which is by no means unique to the Erne and its loughs. However, there is no shortage of breeding birds, which include such species as the great crested grebe, teal and water rail, but there are only smallish numbers of mallard, pochard, tufted duck and goldeneye. Herons, on the other hand, are plentiful and so are cormorants. There are breeding Canada geese on Gad Island and they also winter in large numbers in such places as Inishfendra.

Is it easy to see all of these birds? The brief answer is no. Some of them are usually visible but like all wild life, wild birds are shy of mankind, so patience is needed and not a little perseverance if you are to see anything worthwhile. Such species as the shy garden warbler and its cousin, the grasshopper warbler, are never easy to spot. You may be lucky enough to see the flash of a kingfisher as it whizzes up and down a waterway, uttering its shrill whistle.

Some of the basin's birds are easier to see. The great crested grebe is nearly always actively feeding in the water, and herons, distinctively awkward and upright, are a familiar sight. So also is the sparrowhawk, wheeling over woodlands and fields as he searches for prey. But birds like the shy woodcock are difficult to glimpse.

In recent years a very welcome sight has been the slow floating wheel of the buzzard as it circles over the valleys looking for its prey. The arrival of this bird is an exciting one for the basin, heralding, it is hoped, a change for the better in environmental conditions. Perhaps the faith of the buzzard, in returning to an area from which it has been absent for so many years, is one sign of hope for the rich and varied birdlife of the region.

Belleek China

It has been said of china generally that it is appreciated only by those aged at least forty or over. True or not, it is a saying which cannot be applied to one of County Fermanagh's choicest and most famous products. Everyone, it would seem, loves Belleek china.

What is it about Belleek which is so singularly attractive? It is primarily best known for its translucent glaze and almost pure white qualities. Belleek is distinctive, handsome – but then so are other chinas. What gives it a peculiar distinction is its innately Irish quality; it could never be mistaken for, say, Spode or Royal Doulton. Belleek is, well, Belleek. And there's an end on't.

Porcelain and china are the same thing. China is made in a pottery, baked at a kiln temperature of up to about 1400° centigrade. Its most distinguishing feature is its white-bodied, translucent quality. It evolved in China, which naturally gives it its name, sometime between the T'ang and Sung dynasties of the sixth and thirteenth centuries.

Chinese porcelain, also known as true or hard-paste porcelain, is made mostly from two minerals – kaolin or Chinese clay, and felspar china stone. Peculiarly Chinese for many centuries, it was rediscovered in Dresden in the eighteenth century, an event which sparked off the enormous growth in popularity which china has enjoyed ever since.

Today's porcelain, however, is different from that of the old Chinese porcelain, being slightly harder, a factor due to the input of European potters who experimented with the original Chinese process, changing it as they went along. One of the offshoots of this was bone china, which is a sort of hybrid china which actually contains calcined ox bones – it is still the standard British china today.

Belleek china is again different to this, being a parian china, which is a harder variety invented in the middle of the nineteenth century and used mostly for figures, where its tougher qualities prove ideal. The hardness of parian partly explains why it is possible for the Belleek craftspeople to create such seemingly difficult and intricate work, which hardly seems possible through the medium of clay.

The Belleek Pottery, situated in the County Fermanagh village of Belleek on the banks of Lough Erne and just a few miles from Ballyshannon, was established in 1857 and is Ireland's oldest and most famous pottery. Its visitor centre attracts about 150,000 visitors a year and offers a free guided tour of the factory. Here the visitor can watch the experts in action in such areas as slip-casting, sponging, fettling, basket, mould-making, painting. Every item, whether big or small or in-between, is hand-crafted. All painting is done by hand as well. Particularly popular – and difficult to make – are the famous Belleek interwoven baskets, incredibly detailed. But much else is made here too – plates, cups, saucers, teapots, vases, jugs, figures, photo frames and yes, Irish harps as well.

Belleek china: distinctively Irish

Index